The UNOFFICIAL
Tourists' Guide to
SECOND LIFE

The **UNOFFICIAL** Tourists' Guide to **SECOND LIFE**

Paul Carr &
Graham Pond

B🟦XTREE

First published 2007 by Boxtree
an imprint of Pan Macmillan Ltd
Pan Macmillan, 20 New Wharf Road, London N1 9RR
Basingstoke and Oxford
Associated companies throughout the world
www.panmacmillan.com

ISBN 978-0-7522-2646-0

9 8 7 6 5 4 3 2 1

A CIP catalogue record for this book is available from
the British Library.

Designed and typeset by Andrew Barker
Printed by Bath Press

Visit **www.panmacmillan.com** to read more about all our books
and to buy them. You will also find features, author interviews and
news of any author events, and you can sign up for e-newsletters
so that you're always first to hear about our new releases.

Preface
At the Time of Writing

They say that God made the universe in seven days, including a rather lazy Sabbath. And to this day, there are still some people who believe this to be true. Let's say for the moment that it is. Imagine, then, how ridiculous it would be if on the second day someone came along and wrote a guidebook to the Universe. 'But it's not finished!' God would cry out. 'I haven't even got round to the herbs bearing seed yet, or the fish or the fowl. Or you! How dare you come mooching around here writing guides when I haven't even created you yet?'

Let's say it happened anyway. The point is, if the guide were completed by the morning of the third day, it would be pretty out of date by the end of the week. The universe was evolving so rapidly and would have changed so much in the intervening days as to make the guide obsolete even before it was indexed.

So if the writers of the guide were expecting their book to be anything more than an introduction to a rapidly growing new world, written more as a primer than as a comprehensive study, they were fooling themselves.

And so it is with Second Life.

Thankfully, we know that by the time you are reading

these words, Second Life – which is currently expanding at a rate of 20 per cent a month – will already have left us far, far behind. So what we offer to you today is really nothing more than an introduction to a new world, written more as a primer than as a comprehensive study.

We hope you enjoy it.

Contents

Chapter Five:
Sport, Leisure, and Games 99

Chapter Six:
Shopping and Commerce

Chapter Seven: **Entertainment** 141

Chapter Eight: **Going Native** 181

Chapter Nine: **After Dark** 204

Introduction

Imagine a world in which land can be bought for less than a dollar and the only planning restrictions are those of its inhabitants' imaginations.

Imagine a tourist destination where you awake on your private yacht then spend the morning shopping for virtual designer clothes (created by the real world's top designers) before heading off to a virtual museum for an afternoon of culture (perhaps the enormous Spaceflight Museum with its free rocket trips to Venus, or the sprawling Victorian-themed world of Caledon). Then, after a quick change into your new threads, it's off to a live virtual gig by Suzanne Vega or Razorlight, or a late-night virtual music festival organized (on a specially built island) by the BBC. And if you're still not exhausted (or broke) after all that, imagine a bustling metropolis of over three million people where you can dance the night away in one of hundreds of nightclubs, before perhaps taking a new friend back to your personal spaceship for virtual coffee or . . . well, you get the idea.

With all the possibilities of the real world, minus such irritating restrictions as gravity, taxation, and physics, it's no wonder the world of Second Life, founded in 2003, has proved so popular with virtual tourists. Second Life's population recently passed the three million mark with more arriving every minute, to live or work, or just to check out the sights.

In fact, the only thing that makes Second Life different from a real-world tourist destination is its lack of a decent tourist guide. Until now.

In this book, we provide an unofficial guided tour of the virtually endless wonders offered by this exciting new world. No matter whether you're a Second Life virgin (or 'noob' in Second Life speak), or have been there a while but are looking for fresh stimulation, this guide has something for you.

And like the best guidebooks, this book is also packed with advice on how to make yourself at home. There's advice on what to wear in Second Life and how to act, a guide to the kind of people you can expect to meet, information on how to form lasting (or temporary) relationships with the locals, and, if you decide you'd like to move to Second Life permanently, there are even essential tips on finding – and renting – your first house. All Second Life is here.

We deal in more detail with the geography of Second Life later (p. 30), but in the meantime, a quick word on tracking down the places mentioned throughout the guide. Second Life has a number of ways to refer to specific locations in its world – including Grid coordinates, a website called **slurl. com** that provides direct web links to in-world locations, and a panel in the Second Life software itself providing all sorts of handy search tools. Because of the fluid nature of the Second

Life world, we've stuck to providing accurate, searchable place names that you can type straight into the in-built search tool to jump straight to each location. That way, no matter where a place or attraction may move, you can quickly and easily hunt it down. And to make things even easier, we've also created a website to accompany the book – **http://www.unofficialsecondlife.com**. The site contains direct links to every single place mentioned in the book, including updates if they move. Just visit the site, click your chosen location, and we'll do the rest.

And finally, as we've said, the world of Second Life gets bigger by the day – by the second, even – so if you find a place you think deserves a mention in the next edition of this book, please email it to **change@unofficialsecondlife.com** and we'll do our best to squeeze it in.

Enjoy the book – and make sure you look us up in Second Life!

Paul and Graham
aka Montag Alacrity and Sweetsweet Mincemeat

Chapter One:
In the Beginning . . .

So, what exactly is Second Life?

In a nutshell, Second Life is a virtual world created by computer programmers; a world that you can enter and explore like any other tourist destination, just by logging on via the Internet. Using your keyboard and mouse, you control a graphical representation of yourself on-screen; essentially, it's the natural consequence of those virtual-reality headsets you may have seen on *Tomorrow's World* all those years ago. Now, however, you don't need a headset. All you need is a computer and a broadband Internet connection. Then, if your First Life is not proving particularly satisfactory, to hell with it – you need never leave the house again.

Second Life is an online version of the known world, then, which attempts to replicate many of the basic elements of your First Life – which shall subsequently be referred to as 'Real Life'. Just as in Real Life, Second Life boasts a large and rapidly expanding population, as new users from around the world log on, interact with each other in the virtual space, and, crucially, create new virtual content themselves. Just as in Real Life, Second Life features men and women, land and sky, day and night, flowers and trees. You can build houses and shops, you can work or play, you can make, save, or spend money, you can hang around in bars, watch bands, go on dates, stay at home, read a book, sit, stand, walk, dance, swim, fly, teleport, buy sex organs . . . Ah. Yes, as well as the similarities, there are an awful lot of differences. And just as in Real Life, there is an endless list of activities and opportunities to fill the time between birth and death. Oh, except that in Second Life, death doesn't exist. Or at least not in any significant or lasting way. But more on that later.

Second Life is also like Real Life in one key respect: if you want your life to be worthwhile and interesting, you have to put in a little effort.

Where did the idea come from?

Like many other virtual worlds or massively multiplayer online role-playing games (MMORPGs), Second Life owes much of its existence to the imagination of Neal Stephenson, specifically his 1992 science-fiction novel *Snow Crash*. In this novel, he created an online 'metaphysical universe' called the Metaverse, in which human beings, represented by 'avatars' (a word borrowed from Sanskrit and popularized by Stephenson), could communicate and interact, for business or for pleasure. The fact that Stephenson envisaged this Metaverse even before Web browsers entered the public consciousness is also worth mentioning.

Second Life is not the only virtual world to take its lead

from *Snow Crash* – there are also Active Worlds, There, Dotsoul, and many others. However, Second Life is currently proving by far the most popular, both with ordinary users and, more importantly, with companies wishing to exploit that popularity.

In *Snow Crash*, the Metaverse is a giant black sphere which has a circumference over 1.6 times that of the Earth. Second Life, at the time of writing, is not quite that large. But it's getting there.

Philip Rosedale, CEO of the company responsible for Second Life, also recognizes the novel's influence: '*Snow Crash* has the closest practical resemblance to Second Life as it exists now: a parallel, immersive world which simulates an alternate universe, which thousands of people inhabit simultaneously for communication, play, and work, at various levels and variations of role-playing with their avatars.'

In July 2002, the journalist Wagner James (who, after changing his name to Wagner James Au, went on to become the 'official' reporter of events within Second Life) wrote an article about MMORPGs, posing the question: where are the games that are not solely about killing orcs and trolls or stormtroopers? It seemed that online games would never be able to reach a mass market unless they could appeal to more than bespectacled podgy white boys who were more at home in a medieval forest or a far-flung planet on some imaginary arm of the galaxy than in the real world. Online gaming was all about killing things. It was all battleaxe or laser. Where was the online world that – well, that was slightly more realistic?

Enter Second Life.

Who created Second Life?

Second Life was created and developed by Linden Lab, a San Francisco-based company founded by Philip Rosedale and originally based in Linden Street, from which the name is derived. The story goes that the idea came to Rosedale in the shower. He envisaged a vast virtual landscape distributed across many servers, which people could then inhabit and build upon. Linden Lab went on to make this virtual world a reality.

So how do you play it?

You don't.

Something you must understand from the offset is that Second Life is not a game. From the very beginning, Rosedale declared that his goal with Second Life was to create a whole virtual society, with a functioning and successful economy. 'I'm not building a game,' he said. 'I'm building a new country.'

The idea of Second Life being a game is something many players – or rather, Residents – are particularly uncomfortable with. This is because, unlike gamers, Residents of Second Life have no particular quest to fulfil. There are no levels to go up and no trolls to slay; there is no Death Star to destroy and no evil to vanquish. The point of Second Life – much like Real

Life – is whatever you want it to be, and everything within Second Life is inspired and created by its Residents.

All Second Life really is, is a virtual environment in which Residents can create the world in which they would like to live.

Chapter Two:
The Essentials

OK, so now that we've dealt with what Second Life *is*, it's almost time to hop on a plane and pay a visit. But wait! As with any potentially unstable holiday hotspot, it's wise to spend a few minutes learning a little bit about what to expect before leaving home.

In this chapter, we look at some useful advice for the first-time visitor – what to wear, how to behave, how to stay safe, how money works, the world's official and unofficial news media, and all that jazz.

First Things First

To get to any new tourist destination, you'll need a ticket. In Second Life's case, this comes in the form of the Second Life software that you'll need to download and install before you can access the world. Fortunately for travellers on a budget, this software is totally free. Eat that, Prague!

To download the Second Life software, simply go to **http://secondlife.com**, click the big fat 'join now' link, and follow the instructions. You'll be asked to enter some details about yourself and – excitingly – you'll be invited to choose your Second Life name. On the upside, unlike in the real world, you get to pick the name you enter the world with – no more embarrassing middle names or artily misspelt first names (yes, sorry, we're talking to you, Britnee and Kevan). But on the downside, you have to choose from a list (admittedly very long) of predetermined, often ridiculous surnames, and you can't change your Second Life name later if you realize you've made a terrible mistake.

While researching this book, the authors opted for 'Montag Alacrity' and 'Sweetsweet Mincemeat'. At the time of writing the novelty hasn't yet worn off, but if you see two people with those names lying, wrists slit, under a bridge when you visit Second Life, you'll know we've changed our minds.

The second thing you do, however, says even more about who you are in Real Life and how you want to be perceived in Second Life. The second thing you do is choose your avatar. Initially you are given a choice of twelve ready-made looks, six female, six male, ranging from very ordinary (the girl or boy next door), to very glam (chic or nightclub), to rather exotic (harajuku – improvised Japanese fashion), to alternative (cybergoth), and finally, to furry (furry). Of course once you're inside, you can customize your avatar, or buy or design new parts to be grafted onto yourself at any time, so there's no end to how you can eventually appear; but for a great many Residents, the decision they make on that second Second Life page is the one they stick with throughout their Second Life life. So choose well.

Perhaps the most fundamental decision to make is whether you want to be a human or a furry. The chances are you already know. If the urge to be a furry is within you, you probably knew about it before coming to Second Life. You've probably always known.

You'll notice, when you register, that you have the option to do so as a basic user, or as a paid one. Paid (or 'Premium') users are able to own land, build property, and generally move in to Second Life on a permanent basis. As a tourist, it's best to start off with just a basic account and see how you get on. You might very well hate it.

Having entered your details, and created your account, it's time to download the software to your computer, login, and start exploring. Here we go . . .

Arriving in Second Life: Orientation Island

Ever attentive to the needs of tourists, Second Life's starting point (the equivalent of Second Life International Airport) is Orientation Island. This is the place to orientate yourself within Second Life: to learn how to walk, how to fly, how to interact with others, and how to change the appearance of your virtual self (your avatar) within the world. For your first few minutes in the Second Life world (or 'in-world' as you really should call it if you want to look like a native Second

Orientation Island

Lifer) you'd be forgiven for thinking that someone has spiked your drink. You'll walk into walls, you'll fall off cliffs, you'll find yourself under water, and – embarrassingly – you'll walk headlong into other 'newbies' with no idea how to apologize. Even though your Second Life self is controlled through simple keyboard and mouse commands, it still takes a bit of getting used to (the Second Life software provides lots of help on how to use various features, but in short the arrow keys move you around and the mouse is used to activate more advanced features like teleporting, and using objects).

While on Orientation Island, why not take the opportunity to change your clothes? As you'll see in the 'Shopping and Commerce' chapter (p. 109), there are all sorts of clothing stores to appeal to your inner fashion victim. But even without spending a single virtual dollar you can change your basic clothing, your face, your hair – even your waistline – into something more closely resembling yourself. You can even have spare avatars for different occasions, depending on who you want to be. Montag Alacrity opted to dress a bit like the Fonz would dress if he'd woken up one day without his cool, while Sweetsweet Mincemeat, at the time of writing, is bare-chested, with a skirt and a pink ball-gag.

Then, when you've finished playing and orientating, it's time to get into Second Life proper.

Help Island

Your first stop after Orientation Island should be the equally well-named Help Island. An island designed for newbies to find out what makes Second Life tick – from further customizing your appearance, to using gestures and animations (the cute little bits of magic you can use in Second Life to make yourself dance, or fight with swords or nunchuks, or play chess, or even have really filthy sex), to building your first Second Life home. The fast-evolving nature of Second Life means that any guidebook that attempted to explain all the many possibilities for doing things in-world would be out of date before the ink was dry. However, Help Island is always bang up to date, with Linden Lab employees on hand to answer specific questions. Like any good tourist-information bureau, if you want to get the most out of your visit to Second Life, it's well worth spending some time on Help Island.

Getting Around

There are three main ways to get around in-world. The first is on foot. This is, obviously, a useful way to explore small areas and to meet and interact with your fellow Second Lifers. For people with a good head for heights, the absence of the usual laws of gravity means you can easily fly – Superman style – from place to place. Click the 'fly' button and off you go. Just be careful not to bang your head on any low ceilings. Then again, bang away – it really doesn't hurt and it can be very amusing for others.

The third way is the most useful for those Second Life tourists for whom time is in short supply. It's called teleporting and it allows you to hop directly to any point in Second Life. To teleport, simply use the map or search options in Second Life to find the place you want to visit, and click 'teleport'. Within seconds, as if by magic, you will have arrived. If you have friends in Second Life, you can invite them to teleport to your current location too. No more getting separated or lost!

As you spend more time in-world, you'll find out that there are hundreds more ways to get around, from skateboards and bikes to magic carpets and spaceships.

The Geography of Second Life

Given the ease with which you can teleport around Second Life, it might seem a bit silly to talk about there being any sort of 'geography'. One second you can be standing on the Strip of a virtual Las Vegas and the next you can be in a near-faithful representation of Baker Street underground station in London. But despite time and space being entirely messed up, Second Life can be mapped, like the real world.

The whole of Second Life, taken together, is referred to as 'the Grid', whose daily cycle mirrors Pacific Standard Time. Within the Grid there are various landmasses: three main areas (the Main Continent, the Southern Continent, and Heterocera Atoll), plus various smaller islands – again, not unlike the real world (except that you need to teleport to them, rather than taking a plane or boat). Then within those landmasses, there are smaller regions and cities (often called 'sims'), and within those smaller regions there are individual places – buildings, houses, open spaces; whatever.

While many regions are a mish-mash of different types of buildings and activities, others are more coherently themed. Check out chapter four, 'Key Places to Visit' (p. 68), for more on the weird, wonderful, furthest-flung corners of the Second Life universe.

People

Before going any further into Second Life, a word about its inhabitants. We'll deal with this in more detail in the 'People' chapter (p. 47), but meantime, the first thing that will strike you when you arrive in-world is the diversity of its population. As you'd expect, all creeds and colours are well represented, but don't be shocked if you suddenly encounter a ten-foot-tall robot with shoulder-mounted missiles, or a goblin, or someone dressed as Superman, or a giant devil with claws and wings. Second Life allows a huge amount of customization resulting in a physical diversity unmatched by any place on earth. Even Wales.

However, despite the diversity of appearance, English – specifically American English – remains the language for the vast majority of Second Lifers. Sure, you'll hear a smattering of French or Italian or Spanish – or even Klingon (Geeks! In Second Life! Who'd have thunk it?) – but by and large it's the Americans and the Brits that set the language agenda. (If foreign languages aren't your forte, be sure to download the free Babelfish universal translator, for all your SL translation needs, here: **http://www.slboutique.com/index.php?p=buy &itemid=113720.**)

The easiest way to get to know your fellow Second Lifers is to read their profile information. This is simply a case of right-mouse-clicking on their on-screen avatar and choosing the 'profile' option. If you want to make new friends yourself, then be sure to update your own profile with as much information as you're comfortable sharing.

Fitting In

One of the first things you'll notice when you start exploring Second Life is how friendly (almost) everyone is. Even the oldest inhabitants are barely toddlers in real years and so people are generally keen to get to know each other and to make friends with newbies. As a general rule, no one will object to you using the 'chat' feature to say hello when you arrive at a new place – in fact, it's the polite thing to do. Chatting is simply a case of pressing your return key and typing your words into a chat bar at the bottom of the screen. Most people will say hello back, and unless they're having a private conversation using instant messaging (IM), they'll probably be amenable to a bit of a chat. Likewise, don't be afraid to use the chat feature to ask for help if you need it.

The only thing to be careful of is using the instant-message feature, which allows you to send messages to other Second Lifers that can only be seen by the intended recipient. This is a more intimate form of conversation – the equivalent of whispering – and should only be used sparingly.

As a newbie, you'll also probably find yourself walking into other users as you find your feet. Say sorry, move on – no one will be too offended.

A Two-Minute Primer in Talking Like a Second Life Native

Over time, Second Life has developed its own vocabulary, based loosely on 'net speak'. Mastering the basics of this vocabulary will help you pass as a native quicker than you can say, 'Lol, my hoverboard hasn't rezzed properly. I'm going afk. Brb.' (Tip one: try to avoid saying that; you'll sound fluent, but people will also assume you're an idiot. Or twelve. Or a MySpace user. Or probably all of the above.)

afk – 'away from keyboard'. If someone says this, it means they're going to do something in the real world, like answering the door, or going to the toilet.

av – avatar.

avatar – your virtual representation in the Second Life world; your character on the screen.

beta – the period in a website's development before the full launch, when the site is tested by a relatively small number of users.

brb – 'be right back'. Often used in conjunction with *afk*.

build – the individual properties in Second Life, built by Second Life Residents. A house, a reproduction of the Hoover Dam, and a gigantic shopping mall are all 'builds'.

furries – the non-human avatars in Second Life, most commonly cats, squirrels, and other cute furry animals.

grey goo – the self-replicating objects that sometimes invade Second Life, most famously via a worm released by clicking on the spinning gold rings which one day appeared all over the place.

Grid, the – the continents, islands, seas, etc. that make up the Second Life world.

griefers – Residents whose only pleasure in Second Life is derived from making other Residents' Second Lives a misery. Griefing strategies include trolling (deliberately provoking unnecessary argument), flaming (pretty much the same but generally with more name-calling), and spamming (bombarding users with advertising or other forms of junk).

HI – Help Island (see p. 28).

HUD – a heads-up display (still occasionally 'head-up' display), a virtual version of the HUDs that project useful information onto the helmet visors or cockpit windows of fighter pilots.

IM – Instant Message. Private messages sent to, or received from, other Second Lifers.

in-world – the world inside Second Life. In contrast to Real Life (or RL).

L$ – Linden dollar. The currency of Second Life.

liaisons – The Linden Lab staff who stroll around Second Life (particularly Help Island, helping out newbies).

LOL – 'laughing out loud'. Something which apparently happens with frightening regularity in Second Life.

metaverse – The name often used to refer to the synthetic universe of Second Life.

mouselook – available from the 'view' menu in the Second Life software, mouselook allows you to adjust where your avatar looks by moving your mouse. Some objects (including vehicles) are controlled using the mouselook option.

newbies/noobs – newcomers to Second Life; tourists.

OI – Orientation Island (see p. 26).

poseballs – coloured circles which when activated embed animations into your avatar, allowing it to fornicate with other avatars.

prims (or 'primatives') – the building blocks that everything in Second Life is made of (see 'Going Native', p. 192, for more on prims).

rez/rezzed – as Second Life works over the Internet, and the Internet can be slow, there is usually a gap between you arriving in a new place and that new place appearing properly. In the thirty or so seconds after your arrival, you'll notice buildings slowly take shape, and people, vehicles etc. start to appear properly. This is called rezzing, as in 'man, this place is taking a long time to rez'.

(**being**) '**ruthed**' – this is a rare occurrence in which your avatar, in travelling from one place to another, takes on the appearance of an elderly lady. It's caused by a glitch that confuses you with an early Second Life avatar, who was called Ruth. If it happens to you, consider it an honour.

sandboxes – areas in Second Life where Residents can practise their construction skills.

sim – short for simulator; the regions that make up Second Life.

TG – Teen Grid. Second Life's sister world for teenagers only. (More on that later.)

threads – conversations on Internet forums.

Money

The currency of Second Life is the Linden dollar (L$). Linden dollars can be purchased with US dollars, and can be traded back into US dollars through the 'Lindex' exchange, which puts you in touch with other users who have expressed an interest in buying them. Like any other foreign currency, really. At the time of writing, the exchange rate is approximately L$260 to US$1.

The result of this real-world tradability is that many enterprising Second Lifers have set up real businesses in-world. These range from teenagers creating their own clothing labels and skateboard shops (for Second Life avatars to look cool in and scoot around) to hardcore entrepreneurs selling real estate, spaceships, and even (act surprised) sex and gambling. An oft-repeated story (that may or may not be true) is that some Second Lifers employ workers in the Third World to tend their property and run their businesses in exchange for real dollars, and are simply sitting back counting the profits. Exploitation for the digital age.

Spending Linden dollars is a simple matter, in most cases: click on the item you wish to buy and follow the on-screen instructions. You can also transfer Linden dollars directly to other Second Lifers by pulling up their profile and clicking the 'pay' button.

For more on the shopping opportunities (shopportunities?) in-world, see 'Shopping and Commerce' (p. 109). It's not essential to have money in Second Life, though: according to Linden Lab, only 144,108 Residents spent money in-world in December 2006, and just under half of all transactions were for less than L$20.

Freebies

Fortunately for the tourist on a budget, much of Second Life is still completely free. In 2006 Nissan started giving away Second Life cars to promote their brand in-world. But this being Second Life, they didn't just set up a virtual car-dealership – oh no. Instead they built a giant car-vending machine, which could be used by anyone with a special token. And where did you get these special tokens? From Toast Alicious, a custom-built character, resembling a piece of toast (with eyes and a mouth) that hopped from place to place giving them away, of course. The company also created Nissan Island with a vertical test track to push your new car to its limits. Not to

Free Toyota, anyone?

be outdone, Toyota and GM's Pontiac brand have also opened virtual dealerships, where cars are up for grabs for just a few Linden dollars.

We'll look in more depth at the freebies and paid-for items later in the book, but in the meantime, for some free or almost free goodies, there are no better places to start than the virtual dollar store that is the GNUbie Store or the always free, but often full of rubbish, YadNi's Junkyard.

The Downsides

Reading some coverage of Second Life, you'd be forgiven for expecting a mind-blowing multimedia experience that's so addictive you'll never want to leave and never tire of discovering the exciting sights this brave new world has to offer. And in many ways, you wouldn't be disappointed when you arrived for the first time.

However, let's be honest here, it isn't all plain sailing. One of the first things you'll notice when you arrive is what Second Life regulars call 'lag'. Lag is the gap in time between you using your keyboard or mouse to do something and your avatar on screen actually doing it. At peak times, when tens of thousands of Second Lifers are all milling about in-world at the same time, the lag increases hugely, causing your avatar to jerk about, and then get stuck again, and then to jerk about a bit more like it's having a seizure. Not fun. Think how frustrating it is walking down a busy shopping street at 4 p.m. on

Christmas Eve and you're getting close to the frustration caused by lag.

Linden Lab is always working on ways to speed things up, but in the meantime, if lag starts getting you down, it's a good idea to logoff and come back another time.

Staying Safe

Like the real world, Second Life has a small but growing community of scam artists, who attempt to separate the insufficiently wary from their Linden dollars (which, remember, are convertible into real dollars). Fortunately most scams can be avoided by exercising a little common sense. Before handing over your hard-earned money, ask yourself whether what you're being offered seems – even in a virtual world – too good to be true.

The Big Six Rules

So, yes, Second Life has its fair share of unpleasant elements, but like any good society it has a pretty good system of laws and methods of punishing people who break those laws.

The major crimes – the ones that can get transgressors suspended or even permanently banned from Second Life – are known as the Big Six. They are:

1. Intolerance

In short, this means failing to respect other Residents' race, ethnicity, gender, religion, or sexual orientation. Any open prejudice is dealt with harshly.

2. Harassment

This can take many forms but is defined by Linden as 'communicating or behaving in a manner which is offensively coarse, intimidating, or threatening, constitutes unwelcome sexual advances or requests for sexual favours, or is otherwise likely to cause annoyance or alarm.' As ever, common sense prevails. If you wouldn't say something to someone in the real world, don't say it in Second Life.

3. Assault

This means shooting, pushing, or shoving another Resident in what's termed a Safe Area (most areas in Second Life are defined as 'safe', with a few clearly marked areas set aside where shooting, fighting, etc. are allowed).

4. Disclosure

It's worth remembering that lots of Second Life Residents go in-world to escape from their real lives. With this in mind, Residents are expected to respect the personal privacy of their fellow Second Lifers. It's considered extremely bad form to reveal personal information that you may know about another Resident.

5. Indecency

Although the main Grid of Second Life is only available to over-eighteens, it's important to respect the feelings and sensibilities of other inhabitants. There are some areas where sex, nudity, and all sorts of other adult behaviour is not only allowed, but encouraged. Outside those areas, keep your language clean and your underwear on.

6. Disturbing the Peace

No one likes a troublemaker. Deliberately disrupting live events, bombarding Second Life with advertising, stealing other people's property, and generally making a nuisance of yourself is a quick and easy way to get permanently banned.

For an up-to-the-minute report of criminal action detected in Second Life, and action taken against the criminals, see the official Second Life 'Police Blotter': **http://sec ondlife.com/community/blotter.php**.

Crime

As we have seen, there are things you can do in Second Life for which you can get kicked out. Generally, you have to do something pretty rotten to get more than a warning or a short suspension, but within the Big Six no-nos, there are a great many crimes that an underhanded avatar can commit. A brief glance at the Police Blotter will give you an idea of some of the bad behaviour that takes place. Posting chat logs without full consent of the Residents involved, spamming, trolling, or flaming the forums, making vicious or inflammatory attacks on other Residents, logging into other Residents' accounts and giving away their funds, account hijacking, crude or offensive animations, indecent exposure, and, perhaps worst of all, littering. To name but a few.

Which is all fair enough. It's clear how these activities could upset the smooth running of Second Life, and more importantly, upset the Residents therein.

Obviously, when repeat offenders are identified, they're dealt with and banished. Unfortunately, there's nothing to stop anyone who wants to from merely signing up to Second Life with another identity and committing further crimes. Therefore, other methods of dealing with recidivists have been conceived. For example, there was for a while a Second Life Superior Court, but that didn't really catch on and didn't have the backing of the Lindens. Our favourite punishment, however, was called the Cornfield. If a Resident was sent to the cornfield, every time they logged on their avatar would be trapped on a tractor, going backwards and forwards, condemned to watch an educational film about a boy who turns to a life of crime. A great idea, but again, all the cornfield prisoner had to do was create a new avatar and they were free. (And, indeed, imprisonment in the Cornfield itself became something of a cult objective over time – kids today, eh?)

One of the most notorious criminals in Second Life is Marcellus Wallace. Wallace began his life of crime when he created the Sim Mafia in the game Sims Online. Then when

Second Life became the virtual world of choice, he migrated his Mafia across and began doing favours for Second Life Residents. He is now something of a celebrity in Second Life and likes to think of himself as a kind of virtual Jon Gotti. In Real Life, Marcellus Wallace is an IT specialist called Jeremy.

Second Life News Media

A good way to find out what's happening in Second Life is through the various news outlets that deal with in-world happenings. Some of these outlets are available via the Web, while others actually exist within the Second Life metaverse itself.

If you like your news with added exclamation marks, then the tabloidy-gossipy *Second Life Herald* (**http://www.second lifeherald.com**), the oldest (and arguably still the best) Second Life newspaper, is a great first stop. A nice rival comes in the form of the *Second Life Insider* (**http://www.second lifeinsider.com**) which, as the name suggests, is targeted at the people who live and work within Second Life, rather than casual users and tourists. Elsewhere, the first Second Life newspaper published by a proper traditional media company, Axel Springer's *SL News*, recently started publishing and is delivered by subscription to Second Lifers every day.

In 2006, the Reuters news agency caused a major stir both in Real Life and in-world when it built a virtual headquarters in Second Life, even assigning a dedicated bureau chief, Adam

Reuters (real name Adam Pasick), to cover in-world stories. The Reuters building is a must-visit attraction for news junkies, particularly for the huge, stunning examples of Reuters news photography on the walls and its towering central atrium which, if you fly to the top, allows great views of – well – miles and miles of sea. It's also a great place to meet fellow current-affairs aficionados if you fancy a chat about what's going on in the (real) world. The main attraction, though, is the Reuters heads-up-display (or HUD). Like the HUDs used by fighter pilots to see critical information projected on their cockpits, the Reuters HUD sits quietly in the top corner of your Second Life view, constantly updating with the latest news from the real world. So no need to lose track of what's happening at home.

A Matter of Second Life and Death

For the most part, Second Life – like Disneyland – is a peaceful place where no one dies, there's no violence, and even throwing yourself off a fifty-storey ledge will result in little more than a scratch. Imagine Bill Murray's character in *Groundhog Day*. Now imagine Bill Murray's character in *Groundhog Day*. But it's not all like that. As we've mentioned already, there are areas in-world where violence is not only permitted, but encouraged. If you fancy taking a walk on the wild side, there are a few things to know about killing and being killed in Second Life. Check out the 'After Dark' chapter (p. 204) for more on how to rez some merry hell.

Finally, it's perhaps also worth mentioning here that, when you logoff, your avatar vanishes from the metaverse – but rest assured that he, she or it will be there waiting for you at your home point when you next logon . . .

Chapter Three:
The People

At the time of writing, Second Life is still around the three million Residents mark. That's a lot of people. It can be argued of course that the number of actual, active Residents of Second Life is much smaller. After all, the number of people who join up and figure that the whole experience is about as much fun as wading through treacle, only to logout and never return, must be very high. Second Life can be daunting at first, and for traditional gamers, rather disappointing. However, what makes Second Life worth the time and effort to get to know and use it, is the people that you'll meet when you do. But first, a short history lesson . . .

The History of Second Life, Part One: The Early Days

As with any burgeoning society, things changed quickly in the first couple of years of Second Life's development.

In the very beginning, users were represented not by humanoid avatars but by purple orbs. These quickly evolved into very basic avatars known at the time as primitars, a name taken from 'primitives' or 'prims', which constitute the basic building blocks in Second Life, the stuff from which everything is made. This was back in the day when Second Life was still called LindenWorld, when the landscape was peppered with birds and snakes that fed on abandoned objects, and the early primitars came equipped with guns, grenades, and an energy bar. This was also in the days when there was no currency and no economy. At this stage, it had a great deal more in common with traditional video games. As the concept evolved, however, these gaming elements were jettisoned and Second Life became more reality-based.

As it continued to develop, one of the most important changes in Second Life surrounded the name. To the uninitiated, LindenWorld was fairly meaningless. Other names that were considered included Sansara, a Sanskrit word meaning 'ever-changing world'. Although pleasing to the ear and certainly appropriate, the problem remained that to the outsider – on the fairly safe assumption that your average outsider did not have much of a working knowledge of Sanskrit – it was still fairly meaningless. Eventually, after much debate, Life2 was finally pipped to the post by Second Life. In the words of Linden Lab employee Robin Harper, Second Life was 'more interesting, more evocative and more what we hoped the world could become as it evolved and grew to be as big as life'.

Second Life was opened for public testing in April 2003, by which time it had an early economic system in place in which Residents were charged Linden dollars to create objects.

In June 2003, Second Life went live. And then things really started to change.

In 2006, the history of Second Life was compared by *Wired* magazine to the history of the United States, and there are certainly some similarities. The first period of course is Colonization. This can be said to have begun as far back as spring 2002, when small settlements of 'alpha testers' arrived in Second Life and began to set up camp. As with any new land, rival factions soon established themselves, but it wasn't until around a year later that the first great cultural rift sprang up ... (Go to p. 79 for the History of Second Life, Part Two.)

Groups

Obviously, with such a large number of people represented in Second Life, the variety of interests they bring with them is huge. It can be difficult to find like-minded souls. But just as in Real Life, the Residents of Second Life get around this by forming groups. There are currently thousands of groups in Second Life, from animal lovers (in the nice sense) to animal lovers (in the nasty sense), from would-be philosophers to Real Life knitters to German motor-sports enthusiasts. There are groups for Italians, Koreans, and Scots; groups for Christians, Muslims, and Satanists; groups for alcoholics, gamblers, and perverts; groups for writers, artists, and even Duran Duran fans. (The latter is actually surprisingly popular.) With the caveat that most of what is generally considered illegal in Real Life is also illegal in Second Life, it isn't an exaggeration to say that all human life is here. And then some.

Once you've found a group to which you feel you'd like to belong, all you have to do is click on the 'join' button – unless it's a private club, in which case you're goosed. Then, once you're a member of a particular group, as well as getting to know like-minded people in real time, receiving group instant messages, and having them help you become acclimatized to the new world you have entered, there may also – if the group's any good – be meetings, special events, and so forth. Plus you get a title which is always visible above your name over your avatar's head. This can be whatever the group owners decide – it can be as mundane as Bar Chief or as thoroughly exciting as Flesh Indulger.

Anyone can create a group in Second Life. All you need is L$100 and an idea. The idea doesn't even need to be that good. For example, one Resident set up a group entitled Passed On Animals That We Will Miss. In the group charter – the document that explains why the group exists and what, if anything, it stands for – the owner of the group asked: 'Have you lost a pet and want to share your stories and heartaches with us? . . . Join this group and we won't push you away for being sad.' Two people joined.

But two people is enough. The risk when creating a group – even one where being sad is a prerequisite – is that no one will join; and if no one joins, or if membership falls below two people for as long as a week, your group is dissolved. And you have to live with the shame. Just like Real Life.

In this chapter, we'll be taking a look at some of the most interesting and some of the strangest people that exist within Second Life, as well as some of the weird and wonderful groups they create for themselves.

Furry people

A furry, for the uninitiated, is generally speaking an anthropomorphic animal character. This could be a character from fantasy art, literature, Second Life itself or of course one you make up yourself. The subculture of furry fandom can be traced back to a science-fiction convention in 1980 when Steve Gallacci's *Albedo*, a futuristic comic book featuring over a hundred and fifty humanoid versions of predominantly furry or feathered animals, spawned its own discussion group. From that moment on, furries have gathered together and shared their furry fascination whenever and wherever possible.

According to one furry we spoke to in-world, 'There are several levels of involvement in furry fandom. In my ranking it goes like this: Association, Roleplay (text-virtual), Roleplay (verbal, not Real Life), and finally Suitplay. I classify myself as Roleplay, text.' The Suiters are the ones you may have come across in other parts of the Internet, the ones who dress up and, frequently, have quite a sexual thrust to their love of fur.

Within Second Life, there are seven furry zones, or 'sims', operated by FurNation, a website specializing in furry content: Prime, Alpha, Vista, Aqua, Reia, Omega, and Kitsune.

There is also Luskwood, perhaps the most famous furry hangout. Luskwood will be discussed in more detail in the 'Places' chapter (p. 85), but for now, suffice to say it is utterly charming and inhabited by some of the most affable Second Lifers. On our first visit there, the first thing we heard were the words 'money attack' and we were given L$900 by what appeared to be a giant squirrel.

Famous people

Fortunately there is no Famous People group on Second Life. If there were, it would be, frankly, a bit naff. But that doesn't mean there are no famous people in-world. That's the great thing about virtual worlds: you never know who you're talking to, or dancing with, or kissing or killing. Sure, it could be some spotty kid in Des Moines or Scunthorpe, but it could just as easily be the chubby one out of New Kids on the Block. Then again, when famous people do visit Second Life, they usually do so with something of a flourish, as they're there for a specific reason. Writers, musicians, politicians, academics, businesspeople – all continue to visit Second Life, whether to reach a new audience and experiment with a synthetic universe and an innovative way of communicating, or merely to raise their profile and sell their product. They're often allowed to keep their Real Life surname, so they can be identified in-world.

Celebrity Second Lifers to date have included the writers Kurt Vonnegut, Cory Doctorow, and Warren Ellis; the musicians Suzanne Vega, Duran Duran, and Ben Folds Five; a former Governor of Virginia, Mark Warner; a US Court of Appeals judge, Richard Posner; a leading academic and cyberspace law expert, Lawrence Lessig; Howard Rheingold, the man who coined the term 'virtual communities'; and the man who partly inspired the whole thing, Neal Stephenson.

U2 even appeared towards the end of 2006, although they did so without any kind of actual involvement (see 'Charity', p. 138, in the 'Shopping and Commerce' chapter for more). This was more of a case of Second Life fan fiction. Still, according to some eyewitness reports, this pretend U2 were even better than the real thing.

The emerging celebrities

As well as people who were famous before they arrived in Second Life, of course, there are those who are carving out a name for themselves from the inside out. Probably chief amongst these at the time of writing is Anshe Chung.

In July 2006, Anshe Chung appeared on the front cover of *Business Week* next to the headline 'Virtual World, Real Money'. In November that year she declared herself the world's first Second Life millionaire.

Two and a half years earlier Ailin Graef, Chung's Real Life alter ego, joined Second Life with a $10 account and set about buying and developing real estate. As of November 2006, according to her press release, 'In addition to her virtual real estate holdings, Anshe has "cash" holdings of several million Linden dollars, several virtual shopping malls [and] virtual store chains, and she has established several virtual brands in Second Life. She also has significant virtual stock market investments in Second Life companies.' In short, Anshe Chung became the 'first online personality to achieve a net worth exceeding one million US dollars'. As Wagner James Au points out in his New World Notes, converting all of that virtual money into real money would be no easy task, but on paper – on virtual paper, at least – Chung's claim clearly holds water. It's good to know, however, that she's not just in it for the money.

Says her press release . . .

'Above all, Anshe Chung stresses the importance of community in her vision of the virtual worlds and work spaces that she and others are pioneering together. Her goal is not merely to build a corporation, but to foster the development and growth of online communities, and to help make the entry of real world corporations into Second Life and other regions of the metaverse as frictionless as possible. It is her philosophy that Second Life is above all a social space, and that corporate entrants that respect the community will be the most successful.'

Above all else, however, she has become synonymous with what can be achieved financially in Second Life.

Not far behind her are what are known as the Big Three metaverse commercial successes. These will also be dealt with in more detail in the 'Shopping and Commerce' chapter (p. 109), but for now there is just time to mention Justin Bovington, CEO of London brand consultants Rivers Run Red. In Second Life, Bovington is Fizik Baskerville. Baskerville owns an island called Avalon, which is used not only for promoting his company's clients but also for hosting events such as the Avalon Film Festival and the much-feted Duran Duran concert. Incidentally, Baskerville is also founder of the Duran Duran Fan Club group on Second Life.

It takes all sorts.

Also worth mentioning is a new breed of journalists who are making quite a name for themselves in Second Life. Most important amongst them is Wagner James Au (Hamlet Au in-world), who has been reporting on happenings in the metaverse as Second Life's own embedded journalist since 2003. Very little goes on in Second Life that Au doesn't get to know about, and increasingly, a big story in Second Life is a big story in First Life. It comes as no surprise therefore that Au was one of the editors of the first official Second Life handbook.

Then there's Adam Pasick, who we mentioned in the 'Essentials' chapter. Adam Pasick became Adam Reuters, a full-time embedded journalist for the respected news agency in October 2006. When he was a run-of-the-mill Reuters hack, no one knew who he was. Now he's Adam Reuters, one of an entire virtual world's most important voices. One thing's for sure, he won't be the last.

The Army of Filth

The Army of Filth is a group established by the writer and graphic novelist Warren Ellis. At the time of writing, Ellis is renting a relatively tiny space called Integral Bay, situated in Gibbosa. The idea behind Integral Bay is exploration. Compared to many Second Life sites, on first appearance Integral Bay is not particularly impressive. It looks a little like an abandoned campsite, with huge crates piled haphazardly around the perimeter and a crashed helicopter permanently in flames in the central clearing. On closer inspection, however, it proves to be one of the most original and rewarding areas in the entire metaverse.

The site looks out onto a bay, where a couple of dinghies are laid on for your seafaring pleasure and the back of another unfortunate aircraft juts out of the water. On land, there are more flying machines dotted about the place – usually a couple on top of the largest crate structure. These look like minimalist helicopters but are apparently, according to Ellis's notes for the site, Iron Horses. These are also free for visitors to board and gad about in at their leisure. 'Take them out,' says Ellis. 'Go exploring. The machines will auto-return to me eventually. (Or they'll bug the shit out of someone for all eternity.)'

Elsewhere around the site there are free 'Engine' T-shirts, courtesy of fellow Army of Filth member and celebrated blogger, bestselling author, and London emergency medical technician, Tom Reynolds (Reynolds Horus in-world). There is a reading-room area where for an absolute pittance you can purchase a selection of Ellis's essays and short stories, which incidentally come highly recommended. There are Reuters and Second Life News Network ticker screens; there is free stuff for women, including Superbabes wings, pants, outfits, and jewellery; a fancy little lavatory where your avatar can relieve him- or herself with quiet dignity; and there are the almost obligatory tea crates scattered about the place like cushions. Plus, the music's pretty cool too, streamed direct from the DNA club in San Francisco.

Oh, and one more thing. There is a dinky sim-crossing teleporter which looks like a large lifebelt. This is called the Sender, and with a click and a flush it will transport you to a handful of other Second Life highlights. And despite spending quite a bit of time in Integral Bay, we just bet there's stuff we missed. At the time of writing, Ellis is in the middle of a redesign and in the process of setting up 'informational streams' in the reading area, which he hopes will one day cover the whole of Second Life. We guarantee that by the time you're reading this, there will be a whole host of new features at Integral Bay.

Oh, occasionally there is rain. And always there are birds, which Ellis requests that visitors do not hunt.

Quite right too.

Religious people

With so many people setting up home in another world, it's only natural that many of them are of a religious bent. So, naturally, there are a number of religious-themed groups on Second Life. But probably not as many as you'd expect.

Once upon a time in Second Life, a Resident called Rafin Grimm built a Catholic church. He told in-world reporter Wagner James Au, 'I am Catholic, and very in touch with my relationship with God. I try to be good and do good things. That's what the church was going to be.'

Unfortunately, the general reaction of Residents was not positive. 'I think it is funny,' he said, 'people like having sex clubs and all that here, but you build a church and it is like you are the biggest jerk in the world.'

A similar fate had been suffered by previous places of worship, with Residents complaining that they didn't want to see religion being promoted in Second Life. In one case in particular, however, it was being actively promoted, with a virtual priest handing out T-shirts sporting the slogan 'Jesus had a Second Life, too'.

Back at Grimm's church, even though attendances were fairly healthy, apparently most of the people were friends of his, who also happened to be atheist. Plus, rather than coming to worship, Residents came to debate the existence of God and the place of organized religion. In the end, Grimm took the church down and concluded that society as a whole is becoming less and less spiritual.

Despite this, you can't keep spirituality down, and it will continue to pop up in Second Life. One recent example is a group called the Avatars of Change, which as its founder is keen to point out is not actually a religion, but a culture. According to the Avatarian Charter, composed by group founder Taras Balderdash, the Avatars of Change 'is a group of like-minded seekers of truth who benefit the world. It is a monastic order, as well as a fraternal organization'. Right. Cultures and faiths represented thus far in the Avatarian Way are Zoroastrian, Confucianist, Daoist, Liturgical Christian, Freemason, Jewish, pagan, and Buddhist. Taras is actually represented in-world by a set of eight avatars, each dedicated to a period of Chinese or Mongolian history. And if it's all starting to sound far too wacky to take at all seriously, it's worth pointing out that it does have a serious point and a Real Life application. The AOC collects for charity in Second Life and distributes the money in the real world. So essentially, online charity muggers. But with a heart of gold.

Another church worth mentioning is the First Second Life

Church of Elvis. Floating high up in the air in Iron Fist, the church of the one true King is currently a small-scale affair, decked out with suitably gaudy Presley paraphernalia, including a golden (well, all right, yellow) toilet, free Elvis artwork, pews in the form of purple stretch limos, and a free Elvis pompadour for every worshipper. (Be careful with that pompadour, however. There is the distinct possibility that it may fix itself to your head, never to be removed. Believe us, if there's one thing you don't want, it's to find yourself walking around a Second Life nudist beach in nothing but a pink ball-gag and an Elvis wig. People tend to snigger.) The Right Reverend Elvis Faust, complete with cigar and guitar, conducts the services every Sunday at noon, Second Life Time. They are said to be both poignant and hilarious. To give you a taste, here are the Ten Commandments of the First Second Life Church of Elvis.

1. Thou Shalt Not Take Us Seriously
2. Thou Shalt Take Care of Business
3. Thou Shalt Not Be Cruel
4. Thou Shalt Not Step On My Blue Suede Shoes
5. Thou Shalt Not Kill
6. Thou Shalt Love Me Tender
7. It's Now Or Never – Not O Sole Mio!
8. Thou Shalt Not Build Thine Dreams On Suspicious Minds
9. Viva Las Vegas!
10. Thou Canst Do Anything But Lay Off Of My Blue Suede Shoes!

Other Second Life groups of a religious nature:

Christian Church
Bible studies and sermons for committed Christians. Sermons delivered by Pastor Shadyfox Bellow.

Christians United
'We Basically Hang Out Together and Spread The Good Word'.

Christian Support and Friendship
A group for Christians in Second Life to support one another and make friends. L$10 join-up fee.

Islamic Society

A free group for Muslims. Non-Muslims welcome too.

Buddhists of SL

Buddhists of all traditions, as well as friends of Buddhists. Apparently Second Life offers a unique way to meet others on the path and to spread the Dharma. Also has its own forum. May all be blessed!

Satan's People

'We are dedicated to teaching the writings of Anton Szandor LaVey. We will set a day and time for Satanic bible study when a group is established.'

Political people

As well as the occasional politician jumping on the Second Life bandwagon, many of the Residents are also keen to express their politics within the metaverse.

Although there are surprisingly few groups that represent Real Life political concerns, there are quite a few that are keen to address other important Real Life issues. For example, there are groups supporting animal rights, groups supporting the rights of lesbian zombies, and the Avatars Against Virtual Paedophilia.

But perhaps the most interesting organization within Second Life tackling what it sees as problems within the synthetic society itself is the Second Life Liberation Army. As the name suggests, the SLLA is pretty much the nearest Second Life has to a terrorist organization.

The SLLA was formed as the military wing of a Second Life national-liberation movement. According to its website: 'The movement contends that universal suffrage is a right that should be established within Second Life immediately.' It claims that Linden Lab is operating as an authoritarian government and feels that the only response to this is to fight. Until its demands are met, the SLLA has dissolved the political side of its organization to concentrate on direct military action.

The demands are fairly straightforward. The SLLA believes in in-world voting, and that all Residents must have a say in everything that happens in Second Life. It believes that before any changes are made to Second Life accounts there must be a referendum on each mooted development. Also, crucially, the group feels that Linden Lab should offer Second Life Residents shares in the company. 'We propose that each player is able to buy one share for a set price. This would serve both the development of the world and provide the beginnings of representation for avatars in Second Life.'

Until these demands are met, the SLLA has sworn a campaign of violence against 'the state and other strategically important sites within Second Life'. In-world military operations commenced on 10 August 2006. The next day it 'attacked' American Apparel's in-world store, with SLLA avatars physically preventing customers from buying goods. Since then, attacks on such businesses as Reebok and

Midnight City have continued to be pretty ineffectual, but cash rewards have been offered for any other Resident willing to plant bombs at any of the Big Three Second Life business concerns, Electric Sheep, Millions of Us, or Rivers Run Red (more on those later, in the 'Shopping and Commerce' chapter, p. 109).

There is of course considerable opposition to the SLLA's tactics, most of which centres on the fact that Linden Lab is a company and that as such it can do what it damn well likes. If you don't like it, say those opposed to the SLLA, go set up your own virtual world. But then the response to that is surely that from the very beginning, Second Life was always going to be so much more than a game and a business – it was going to be a fully functioning online society. And a crucial part of any society is dissent.

At the time of writing, more attacks are planned and representatives of Linden Lab are naturally unwilling to give in to terrorism. Who is? So this one will either run and run, or else the Lindens will simply wait till the SLLA does something offensive enough, and then ban it.

The SL Alliance

As with anywhere else on the Internet – and indeed in Real Life – there are always going to be some people who just want to ruin it for everyone else. In Second Life, these people are known as 'griefers'. Their typical behaviour can be the obvious annoyances like trolling, flaming, killing, and so on, but they can also make a nuisance of themselves by dropping stuff in your inventory, hassling you, getting in your way, and generally stopping you doing whatever it is you're trying to do.

These people are a problem not just personally, but also for the trouble they cause the game as a whole. Games publishers have calculated that as much as 25 per cent of all customer-service calls are down to complaints about griefers. That's a lot of wasted effort and a lot of wasted expense. Plus there's the problem that the more frustrated other Residents get, the more likely they are to stop using the game.

But what can you do? It's the age-old problem of what to do about the ones who ruin it for everyone.

In 2005, following a massive amount of grief at three of Second Life's main sandboxes, Goguen, Cordova, and Newcomb, a group of Residents decided it was time to take things into their own hands. And so, intent on putting a stop to the destructiveness of these griefers, the Alliance was born. Quickly amassing around forty members, many of whom had Real Life military experience, the Alliance built enormous ships which they stationed around the affected sandboxes. The idea was to be able to supervise the sandboxes and protect them against abuse.

Although opinion is very much divided on the necessity of what is essentially a self-appointed volunteer vigilante force, the Alliance counter that they are absolutely necessary, as the official police force of Second Life, i.e. the Lindens, were simply not up to the task. Alliance member Eric Groshomme told the *Second Life Herald*, 'They take over twenty minutes to respond, sometimes an hour. We're there in minutes.' Many other Residents have complained that the Lindens are not necessarily the best at dealing with abuse within Second Life. There are stories of Residents reporting someone to the Lindens, and receiving a standard form reply claiming that the problem has been resolved, but then nothing appears on the Police Blotter to prove that it has.

In October 2005, the Alliance moved out of the sandboxes and set up a more permanent home in Enceladus. Part of the reason they left was because Residents were reporting them for griefing. What goes around comes around.

Chapter Four:
Key Places to Visit

In the future, entire guidebooks may well be written for specific areas of Second Life – *The Virtual Guide to Second Life Dublin*, for example; *The Luskwood Baedeker*. But for now, what follows is a brief guide to some of the more interesting and fun places you should visit.

Before we get going however, a little advice about getting around. Pressing your ctrl and F keys in Second Life brings up an incredibly useful search panel. One of the tabs on this panel, marked 'Popular Places', features a list of the most popular places in Second Life. Typically, this list will be dominated by a list of seedy-sounding places, many of which have asterisks or exclamation marks in their name, and most of which are places to gamble and places to watch naked people dancing. This, we presume, is because no matter where you go, First Life, Second Life, and no doubt even the After Life, most people are still fairly degenerate and slave to their baser desires.

However, these places are not – generally speaking – very good. They're the kind of places that deal with and exploit lowest-common-denominator urges, so they're fairly tacky, and tawdry, and tend to attract a certain shabby type of person. As in Real Life. So we're not going to be talking much about those. We may mention them in passing, but only rather disparagingly, comparing them unfavourably with the much classier places we'll be describing in detail.

Amsterdam

Like its real world equivalent, Second Life Amsterdam is a veritable hotbed of iniquity and murk. And bicycles. Lots and lots of bicycles. Aside from being one of the main sex-trade centres in-world (more on that in the 'After Dark' chapter, p. 204) and the best place to pick up some genitals for your avatar (ditto, see also the 'Shopping and Commerce' chapter, p. 136), it boasts some stunning scenery. Realistic-looking

bridges and boardwalks line the canals, while several of real-world Amsterdam's historic churches have been faithfully recreated. In fact, were it not for the fact that the place is basically one huge red-light district, where you can actually *hear* people having sex when you walk past buildings, it'd be a lovely place to take the family for a day trip. Ah well. We'll always have Paris. Or, in Second Life's case, Paris Island, which isn't quite the same.

Nexus Prime (Gibson)

Fans of the cyberpunk lifestyle, such as that described in the books of William Gibson, will want to visit Nexus Prime, a

city of futuristic buildings, hovercars, people who look like robots, and – of course – a vending machine that allows you to download sample chapters from Neal Stephenson's *Snow Crash*.

When you first arrive, you'll be struck by how polished everything is. Skyscrapers stretch upwards as high as you can fly and amazing futuristic transport machines whiz past above your head. This is the future, for sure. But wander off the main drag, beneath gleaming streets, and you'll realize that things aren't all that they seem. Below the surface you'll soon find mazes of rusting steel and decaying graffiti-covered concrete, while cyberpunk Residents skulk about, looking futuristically suspicious of your presence. A great place to buy skater wear and virtual tattoos, too.

Svarga

The future is a great place to visit – but if you're after something more spiritual, you can't go far wrong with Svarga.

In Hinduism, 'Svarga' is a kind of temporary Paradise. It is a place where the righteous souls of those who led virtuous lives reside until they move on to their next physical incarnation. As such, with its heavenly connotations, it is a fitting description of a Second Life island created by Resident Laukosargas Svarog.

What makes Svarga special is that it is the only place in Second Life with its own fully functioning ecosystem. In

Svarga, clouds that rain real rain are blown across the sky. When given the right amount of rain and sunshine, flowers grow and are pollinated by bees that in turn are occasionally picked off by hungry birds. As in Real Life, the entire ecosystem is interdependent. Without the clouds, the plants would die; without the plants, the bees would die, and so on.

Svarga is one of the most beautiful places in the whole of Second Life. Go there and take the tour and you will be transported round the island in something like a large half shell, which will carry you through what feels like a tropical rainforest on a particularly exotic planet. You will float past mountains, palm trees, waterfalls, and what appear to be giant fungi. You will feed the birds, play with other avatars in the castle, take part in sound experiments that generate music from chat, and at the end of it all you will feel cleansed.

After which, if you're a fan of Laukosargas Svarog's work, you must make a visit to Lauk's Nest. Again, there is some jaw-dropping scenery, best of which, high in the air built around the trunk of an enormous tree, is a platform with a bunch of percussion instruments – drums, gongs, congas, a rain stick, and so on – which you can play in sync. Above this impromptu music stage is the most adorable tree house you ever did see.

The Blarney Stone, Virtual Dublin

Virtual Dublin

Sticking with the theme of dragging real-world things kicking and screaming into Second Life, it seems that Residents just can't resist replicating their home cities in-world. Virtual Dublin is an excellent example of this, offering as it does a lovingly built representation of the Irish capital's city centre. Points of particular interest include the Guinness factory (a bit bare at the time of writing, but good things come to those who wait), Trinity College, and the Temple Bar area. And of course, this being Dublin you'll want to pop into the Blarney Stone, a traditional Irish pub – or at least traditional in the sense that it serves absinthe and plays Bruce Springsteen on the radio. Oh and it's packed with Americans. Still, it's also without a doubt the best place in Second Life to play a quiet game of darts (follow the bar round, across the dance floor, and into the back room).

Camp Darfur

Not all the virtual representations of the real world in Second Life are designed for fun. Camp Darfur is Second Life's very own refugee camp, created to raise awareness of the plight of the people forced to flee their homes in the troubled region of the Sudan.

The first thing you notice when you arrive is the fire.

Everything is ablaze – the camp is 'decorated' with simulated flames, and weapons and skulls litter the ground, reminding visitors that the camp is the product of violence and murder. And if the message wasn't clear enough, there are links to the websites of aid agencies working in the area, and a huge poster reminds us of the daily death toll in the region. There are even giant video screens showing interviews with real Sudanese refugees telling their stories. If you want to show your support for the cause, you can even pick up a free T-shirt or wristband to wear in-world. A great example of how Second Life can be used to raise awareness of a serious issue.

Neufreistadt

One for the political scientists, Neufreistadt is an attempt to bring local politics into Second Life. The town has its own system of elected government, the Representative Assembly, which serves for six months between elections. The Assembly is responsible for passing laws, which all inhabitants of the town agree to abide by or face being banned. There is also a judiciary, a scientific council, a civil service, and even a union representing the town's artisans. For more about the town and how it works, see: **http://history.secondserver.net/ index.php/Neufreistadt**.

Pomponion Volcano

The Pomponion Volcano is notable for two reasons. One, for its active volcano, bubbling hot lava out of the ground and pouring across the surrounding rocks. And two, for its enormous towering skyscraper looking out across said volcano. Now, while one might question the wisdom of building a skyscraper on top of an active volcano, there's no arguing with the incredible results. For a truly unique-to-Second-Life experience, teleport yourself up to the viewing platform at the top and then swoop down over the crater. And for an even bigger thrill, why not have a paddle in the volcano itself? When we did, we were surprised to find a quad bike nestling at the bottom, like a supermarket trolley at the bottom of a canal.

Nakama

The island of Nakama brings together Second Life and the world of Japanese animation. Developed by Neil Protagonist (a surname familiar to *Snow Crash* enthusiasts), the island consists of multiple districts (or *ku*s), each with its own distinct look, reflecting a different aspect of the Japanese animator's art and with billboards showing examples of cartoons. There's also a commercial side to Nakama – in fact it's part island and part enormous shopping mall. Most of the items – from the buildings to the lampposts – are for sale simply by clicking on them. Then it's just a case of installing your new purchase on your own virtual land (see 'Going Native', p. 185) for others to admire.

Jessie

Abandon hope all ye who enter here. While in most of Second Life gun ownership and wanton violence are banned, in Jessie it's pretty much mandatory. Like a virtual Wild West, Jessie lies behind the Jessie Wall, once a physical barrier, but now more of a conceptual one at which point the law stops and anarchy reigns. Gun shops litter the streets, many offering free weapons (we picked up a rather cool watermelon launcher), while all around the place are splattered American flags. Jessie is also, however, famous for its part in the so-called Jessie Wars, ugly periods in Second Life history that many Residents have likened to the wars in Iraq. As a result, perhaps it's not surprising that most of the people you'll find there are American. And pro-war. If that bothers you, stay away – or at least make sure you're packing serious heat . . .

The History of Second Life, Part Two: Second Life War One

April 2003 – groups of players of World War II Online (WWIIOL) began to arrive in Second Life. WWIIOL is another massively multiplayer online role-playing game, wherein, according to its website, you will find 'a mixture of hard-core, pulse-pounding action, stealth, strategy and team-work'. It's a war game, essentially, played by war buffs – many of these are military or ex-military in Real Life, many of them just gun nuts, many of them merely massively into the idea of combat and killing. These war gamers began to arrive in Second Life as their own game forums had become overrun by anti-war protesters – these were Real Life anti-war protesters, against the war in Iraq and taking out their frustrations on a bunch of online gamers. So many of them drifted over into Second Life and set up shop in the Outlands, an area of Second Life designed specifically for combat.

In the rest of the metaverse, any kind of combat is strictly forbidden, falling within the remit of the Big Six behavioural no-nos (p. 40). Shooting people with enormous Tommy guns falls down in at least four or five of those categories.

However, by the time the World War gamers arrived, the Outlands, due to a land crisis in the rest of Second Life, had become inhabited by Residents keen to set up ordinary non-combatant homesteads with the hope of living ordinary peaceful lives. But this wasn't to be.

The first wave of WWIIOLers created their own group within Second Life and set to work building authentic WWII weapons and buildings. Despite their military obsessions they seemed really surprisingly peaceful, concerned rather with creation and socializing rather than with out-and-out carnage, and were accepted by other established Residents. Their arrival, however, was reported on IGN, a hugely popular gaming website. This report then prompted a second wave of WWIIOLers, which was when the trouble started.

In *New World Notes*, his online journal documenting the social evolution of Second Life, embedded journalist Wagner James Au notes that the ensuing battles coincided with a particularly fraught period in the war in Iraq. It was in March that coalition forces toppled the statue of Saddam Hussein and President Bush announced plans to launch a 'decapitation strike' at Hussein and his family. These were anxious times, and the WWIIOLers needed some kind of catharsis.

What followed has been described by Outlands Residents as an out-and-out invasion. Combat-hungry WWIIOLers arrived and immediately stocked up on virtual weaponry. One in-world arms manufacturer is said to have earned tens of thousands of dollars in a week.

Once armed to the teeth, the WWIIOLers embarked on a killing spree.

Every Resident in Second Life must establish a home point. Naturally, Residents who choose to build homes tend to set their home points there. Makes sense. There's no place like home. Your home point is the place to which, should you become lost, disoriented, or just plain homesick, you can always teleport. It is also the place to which you return if you happen to be killed. What this meant, then, was that during the upheaval of the WWIIOL invasion, many peaceful Outlands homesteaders were killed in cold blood, reincarnated, and returned home where their murderers were waiting for them to kill them all over again. Which has got to be annoying.

It was the WWIIOLers' unashamed aim to take over the Outlands using extreme violence. Some of the Outlanders decided to fight back, however, and a great battle ensued.

Even though originally the Outlands were all about combat, things had changed and the new era of hostility was clearly out of hand. As a consequence, many Residents complained to the Lindens. 'Attempting,' as Wagner Au puts it, 'to act as a kind of United Nations', the Lindens stepped in and decreed that three of the four Outlands land masses (or 'sims') were designated 'no-kill' areas. From this point on (the summer of 2003) open hostility was restricted to the Jessie simulator, which was encircled by a giant, would-be impenetrable wall. This however, was far from the end of the troubles.

The war in Iraq, which continued apace, saw a parallel inside Jessie. WWIIOLers, Outlanders set on revenge, and all other Second Lifers with hostility issues gathered together and murdered each other with increasingly technologically advanced alacrity. It also became a battleground where people with differing opinions about the Real Life war antagonized one another. The wall surrounding Jessie was daubed with pro- and anti-war statements and images. So as well as physical violence, a propaganda war ensued.

The propaganda war culminated when one Resident, Syank Nomad, began posting Confederate flags about the place. The Confederate Naval Jack was considered by many a symbol supportive of slavery. A debate ensued as to whether Nomad should therefore be expelled from Second Life for breaching the rules against 'hate speech'. Finally, the Lindens stepped in again and fixed the Jessie wall so that nothing more could be attached to it. Not everyone was pleased by this but it did bring an end to the first great Second Life war, which was in itself an amalgam of World War II, the Second Gulf War, and the American War of Independence.

And synthetic world wars don't get much more controversial than that.

Wengen

In Wengen it's winter all year round. Although the ski lift in Second Life's premier ski resort didn't seem to be working when we arrived, it's a simple matter to fly up to the highest peaks and enjoy the view of . . . well . . . snow as far as the eye can see. And for those in need of a bit of alpine athleticism, the lower peaks of Wengen – for reasons not entirely clear – also play host to fencing tournaments. The perfect place to get away from it all. Do wrap up well, though.

The Lost Gardens of Apollo

Born of an inspiration to create an alternative to the garish carnality in Second Life, Danish Resident Dane Zander sought to build an adult environment that was focused on mystery and a more thoughtful, seductive eroticism. As with a (perhaps surprisingly large) number of places in Second Life, the accent here is on the romantic and the tender, rather than the buck-naked and gyrating.

The Gardens were based on those to which Apollo used to take his gay lovers, according to the myth of Apollo and Hyacinth. Apollo was so keen on Hyacinth that he even named a flower after him, and Zander's tribute to Apollo's devotion, and indeed to his gardens, is easily one of the most beautiful places in the whole of Second Life. Mountains, pyramids, architecture as exotic as you could ever hope to see. Incredibly delicate structures with towers that shoot up endlessly into the clouds occasionally give way to seemingly floating, totally secluded, and perfectly intimate stone pools. It reminded us of a slightly more Eastern version of Cappadocia in Turkey, with its landscape dominated by giant 'fairy chimneys', sculpted from the volcanic rock over centuries. Only this is somehow better. It has rather a lot more to offer.

Swoop down through the clouds at dawn, glide between the legs of the giant statues of Apollo and Hyacinth, plunge into the bay, and stop for a moment at the sharpened riblike teeth of the giant pilot fish therein. Or take a tour at sunset, where everything takes on the sultry glow of a dark orange moon. In its way, sunset is even more astonishing. It's just that you don't get to see as much.

There are donation boxes scattered around the Gardens, and you might well think, without having been there, why on earth would I give someone money to play all day on a computer, making castles in the air? Your cynicism is understandable. But come to the Lost Gardens of Apollo and button it. The Gardens are a testament to what can be achieved in a virtual world. What they lack in physical reality, they more than make up for in every other respect.

There were moments exploring the Gardens of Apollo where this virtual man in a skirt genuinely had to catch his breath. It's the kind of place where at the end of a day's exploring, you find yourself saying, 'You need at least a week.' But you could probably spend your entire Second Life here and never tire of its beauty.

Luskwood

Created in mid-2003 and currently stretching to over 100,000 square metres, Luskwood is Second Life's oldest furry-themed area. It consists of two sims, Lusk and Perry, with a degree of overlap into Clara. Owned and run by the Luskwood Group, it is also home to Luskwood Creatures, the first company to set up in the furry-avatar business (p. 124). Each area of Second Life has a rating – either Mature or PG. Luskwood is rated PG, and is generally considered the decent, responsible, and, ironically, mature face of furry fandom.

Generally speaking, furries have something of a reputation for being wary of outsiders (non-furries). This stems from an often intolerant, suspicious, or downright weirded-out attitude towards furries from their non-furry counterparts. The Residents of Luskwood, however, have no such qualms and non-furries are as welcome in Luskwood as they are anywhere. Indeed, special events are often held in the area's beautiful, natural, and predominantly non-commercial landscape, to which all, but specifically non-furry Residents, are invited.

Luskwood is typified by creativity, generosity of spirit, and fun. It's no surprise then that the first feature-length film to be screened in Second Life was in Luskwood. It's also perhaps no surprise that that film was *Godzilla 2000*, a lavishly animated Japanese version of the classic tale of a really quite loveable dinosaur. It's also home to much-loved annual events, such as their Easter Egg Hunt and New Year Party, where avatars and Linden dollars are given away at random.

Luskwood: there may be no nicer place in the whole virtual world.

Virtual Hallucinations

Despite the many adult themes in Second Life, not many of the places you can visit actually come with a medical warning. Virtual Hallucinations does.

'Some people find the Virtual Hallucinations experience disturbing, particularly the voices. If you find it bothersome, just walk to the end of the clinic and click the "Stop Voices" button.'

Virtual Hallucinations is one of those projects in Second Life which have clear ideas about how experiences within synthetic worlds might be used to improve our understanding of life in the real world. Devised by computer scientist and former physician James Cook, Virtual Hallucinations is a tool for educating people about mental illness – in particular schizophrenia. In the past, being educated about mental illness – or indeed anything else – was often a very dry, wordy experience. One of the great potentials of Second Life, however, is its ability to educate in a highly interactive, synaesthetic, kinaesthetic, and above all enjoyable way. Therefore in Second Life discovering schizophrenia can be really quite a personal and disturbing voyage.

Essentially, Cook has attempted to include in his project all the paranoia and disorder, and all the aural and visual hallucinations of the real thing. Based on the real hallucinations of two actual schizophrenia sufferers, the clinic is designed to give an accurate representation of how intrusive the voices actually are. For the full effect of the tour it is recommended that you switch your view to mouselook. This gives you much greater involvement. You're not watching an avatar on a screen. You *are* an avatar, and you're walking through a clinic

going quite, quite mad. Personally we would also recommend you wear headphones.

As you enter the deserted clinic where the Virtual Hallucinations Tour takes place, you click on a disc and embed the 'voices' animation in your avatar's mind. Then, with the voices drifting in and out of your consciousness – 'Kill yourself,' they hiss. 'Do it. What the hell. Go on, do it.' – you walk through corridors and into deserted rooms. As you go, everyday objects turn against you. Words on a poster and in a newspaper change to insult or incite you. In a mirror on the wall a reflection that isn't quite yours slips in and out of focus, returning to clarity with an anguished expression and bleeding eyes. The voices stay with you throughout, ever more insistent. 'You're not sick. You're not really unwell. We only have so many beds . . . You're nothing. You're worthless. You're the most worthless person in the world and I won't have you damaging my society. Kill yourself now . . . You don't even exist. You're just an illusion.' Intermittent bagpipe music makes the experience all the more unpleasant.

As Dr Cook says, please do be careful. And remember, unlike Real Life schizophrenics, you can put an end to the torture any time you like.

Roma

Ave, Citizen!

From the Roma notecard: 'This is an ancient Roman themed sim. Torin Golding designed it, built it, and owns it. The sim is managed by the Emperor Julian Augustus. Roleplaying a member of the ancient Roman empire is welcome in Roma, although certainly not required of all visitors. All visitors and Citizens are expected to abide by the Emperor's rules of conduct while in the sim. A copy of these laws is available in the back room of this Customs House and also under the estate's Covenant tab.'

It took Torin Golding quite a while to develop his Second

Life Roma to the spectacular city with its very own sim that you can visit today. It wasn't built in a day, that's for sure.

Second Life Roma is like an amalgamated metaversion of the original city. Most visitors arrive via the main portal into a town square where they can experience many of the sights and sounds you may well imagine when you picture a typical Roman public space – the bustle of a street market, a tavern, a theatre, a room for games, an arena for gladiators, and even a Roman baths.

Alternatively, it is just possible that when ancient Rome comes to mind, you skip all that and concentrate solely on the orgies, the eunuchs, the virgins, and senators marrying their horses. Well, Roma has that too, and most of it quite rightly is concentrated in Caligula's Pleasure Palace.

There are also chariot races in which Residents compete against one another; there are extensive bath houses at which free towels are provided; there are mosaics, lions, and a not-to-scale model of the Pantheon. And of course, all of the excitement, skulduggery, and intrigue of Ancient Roman politics, as played out by anyone who has a yen to pretend.

Vampire Empire

As we've seen, role-play is of primary importance within Second Life. In fact, it's not uncommon to find yourself playing more than one role at once. For example, you can be an ordinary person in the real world pretending to be an

ordinary person in a virtual world pretending to be a Roman gladiator. How seriously these roles are taken is obviously left entirely up to the individual. Some people take them very seriously indeed, with an attention to visual and verbal detail that can be quite disconcerting. Some of these people are vampires.

'We're sex,' one Second Life vampire told the *Herald*. 'We're the act of violation. We're rock-star gods . . . The Vampire life is a shot at immortality, it's a shot at something bigger than yourself. Some people want to be vampires because it's a somewhat exclusive club. Others want to be vampires because it gives them an excuse to indulge in their basest desires.'

So there you have it.

Vampire Empire, however, according to its creator Obscuro Valkyrie, is not about role-play. 'This is our subculture,' he says, 'not an Internet game where you bite people.' Created in 2003 as a safe haven for all those of a vampiric bent, Vampire Empire moved to its own island a year or so later. Centred around a beautiful castle, Vampire Empire offers a 'dedicated active Gothic scene, strong Vampiric style, obscure music, interesting curiosities [and] Goth/Industrial clothing'. When we first arrived there, we were witness to what appeared a very sedate village dance. Quite charming.

Obscuro Valkyrie is also, according to groups he has joined, a Second Life Buddhist, Hippy, DJ, and Son of a Bitch. You have been warned.

Transylvania

Transylvania has everything you might expect. Towering dark castles, damned bloodless souls, a museum charting the history of vampirism, and an overwhelming sense of impending doom. But there are also shops!

Even so, it's probably not an ideal place for a first date, unless your first date happens to be some pale-skinned wannabe blood doll. In which case, yes, bring them here.

Gor

Another Second Life sim big on role-play is Gor. Gor is based on the 'Chronicles of Gor' by the American writer John Norman, a series of twenty-six novels which combine science fiction, philosophy, and erotica. Gor is the name of the world on which each of these novels is set, a distant planet on the other side of the Sun from the Earth, a world where men are very much the dominant sex and women for the most part are chattels. Consequently there is a fair bit of domination on Gor, and a fair bit of submission. So, naturally, Gor fans are very drawn to the Second Life version of Gor, where they can freely indulge their sub-dom fantasies, allow themselves to wear collars and chains and submit to the absolute power of another human being, without ever having to leave their house in Scunthorpe or Des Moines.

In Second Life Gor, there are different levels of Gorean. There are those who call themselves Full RP Goreans. These are full-on disciples of the Books of Gor. They role-play situations and stories in the books and never leave the Gorean sim. Then there are those who are a few degrees less insane who recognize that there is more to Second Life than sexual slavery.

There are also Panther women, who in the books were able to escape the city walls and live in the surrounding forests. In Second Life, these Panther women have evolved into a more dominant kind of Gorean female, a subculture of Amazonian queens who will dominate just about anyone.

We spent a little time in Turia, one of the main cities of Gor. Hail!

Read the rules of Turia before you start wandering around or you could be in for something of a surprise. Although the rules declare that Turian life is a 'rich tapestry of honour, duty, and passion' and that 'Turia prides itself on the beauty and temperament of her slaves', it also confesses that 'sex and violence (and violent sex) are as normal and legal here as church on Sunday in the United States'. So be careful out there.

As well as human beings in Turia, there are also Priest-Kings, Kurii, and Spider-People. Priest-Kings and Spider-People are likely to be attacked on sight, apparently, so if you do see one, get stuck in there. They'll be half-expecting it. You will be pleased to hear however, that there are no 'talking larls, sleen, urts, or tarns'. Although we have no idea what these things are, we can't help feel that their absence is a good thing. Nothing worse than getting stuck in conversation with a dreary sleen. We imagine.

If you're not actually playing a role in Turia, and therefore are not dressed in typical Gorean garb, it is advisable to wear an Observer tag, otherwise it is quite likely that, as well as calling you a barbarian, someone may well try to capture and snap a collar on you. Also, if you're not wearing an Observer tag, you are expected to be in character at all times. If you're not, expect to be dealt with severely.

Having said all that, we bought a couple of sexy silks in harem pink and a beautiful sheer veil, but still we couldn't find anyone willing to dominate us. But then, as it says in the rules, 'If you come seeking to find sexual gratification you will be sadly disappointed. Nothing in life worth having or living is without effort. Learn what it is that you want and grow within your role.'

Bah. Still, if role-playing and sub-dom and violent sex are what you're into, do pop along and make the effort. You may well be handsomely rewarded.

Dark Life

Another role-play and gaming paradise for Second Lifers is Dark Life, set on the once-peaceful island of Navora.

When you arrive at Dark Life, you are expected to familiarize yourself with the rules of the game and buy yourself a backpack which contains the code, and some starter weapons. The story of the game of Dark Life was summed up in the *Second Life Herald* as 'everything was fine and then the monsters came', which is pretty much all you need to know.

Then, using your weapons, armour, potions, and spells, off you pop into good old-fashioned Dungeons and Dragons-style combat. As in D&D, you can form teams (with the help of a group bracelet) and, as your experience grows, go up levels.

If you do go to Dark Life, we recommend that as soon as you've got yourself a pocketful of gold, buy yourself a Staff of Pain. They're cool.

Intimate Moments

The co-owner of Intimate Moments in Polia is Bam Camus. Bam describes her creation as 'a romantic garden with opportunities for kiss, cuddle and more, offering a unique and classy way to enjoy a virtual relationship'. Indeed, although there are areas within Intimate Moments in which couples hire a room to watch dirty movies together, this is a long way from the seedy atmosphere of places such as Amsterdam and some of the malls that specialize in animal genitals. At Intimate Moments, the accent is most definitely on Romance.

When Bam Camus first came to Second Life, her intention was to build something unique and connected with personal relationships. 'I think that before sex comes romance. Our entire ground is devoted to romance . . . You can come here and relax, get to know someone, without the idea that you're a piece of meat waiting to be eaten. We have 40,000 square metres with tons of secluded areas where couples can chat while cuddling or kissing. We have two public sex areas that are off the ground and three themed private rooms.' One of these rooms is a garden, one a luxury suite, and the other a castle dungeon. 'We also have a rustic woods setting for members only.'

We'll come back to love and sex in the 'Going Native' and 'After Dark' chapters, but in the meantime, a trip to this romantic garden is highly recommended. Go and practise your seduction techniques and see if you can get someone who takes your fancy to share some intimate moments with you. Obviously, it's very odd – if not downright creepy – to speak of kissing and cuddling and romance and interpersonal relationships when really you're just a bunch of pixels on a computer screen. However, once you've clicked on the kissing scripts at Intimate Moments and seen your alter ego in a passionate tongues-and-groping clinch with another avatar, then you may begin to understand it. Alternatively, you may not.

Teen Second Life

One major area of Second Life that is beyond the scope of this book is Teen Second Life, otherwise known as the Teen Grid. The Teen Grid is entirely separate from the main Second Life world, and it's developed for thirteen-to-eighteen-year-olds. Designed to protect teenagers from the more adult aspects of Second Life, this is a heavily policed environment where all but the most innocent of behaviour is banned and characters are expected to behave themselves at all times.

One amusing aspect of the Teen Grid is the ban on avatars removing their underwear, to enforce the no-nudity rules there. Of course, teenagers being teenagers, Residents quickly worked out that the rule could easily be circumvented by creating special underwear and clothing that was transparent. Kids today, eh?

If you feel slightly peeved that you're being excluded from

something that might be quite fun, it's probably worth bearing in mind these words from Teen Second Lifer Elitesniper223 Qin, as reported in *New World Notes*: 'The teen side of Second Life is, sadly, for the most part what you'd expect. The majority of the population is either inactive, not creative, lazy, or just plain ignorant. The economy is based majorly [on] rip-offs from real life, "bling", freebies, and teen Second Life's idea of a multigadget . . . While there are some nice, intelligent, and clever people, the population is riddled with people that are trying to be "gangsta", that are constantly copying other people's ideas, and that are just plain stupid . . .'

So perhaps it's no bad thing that you can't get in there.

For more on the Teen Grid, see **http://teen.secondlife. com**.

Chapter Five:
Sport, Leisure, and Games

There is, if you'll forgive the irony, no shortage of outdoor activities to enjoy in Second Life. From aeronautic exhilaration to a leisurely round of golf, you'll be spoilt for choice.

Abbotts Aerodrome

Up, up, and away! Abbotts Aerodrome is the place to go if you have a head for heights and a taste for adventure. If you're visiting on a budget, arrive early to beat the crowds and then head to the top of the skydiving tower. Ignore the sky shop for now and instead head straight for the skydiving deck, which offers a free jet-powered chair thing which will launch you up to 4,000 feet above the ground for a dramatic near-space freefall.

While you can't feel pain in Second Life, if you want to make the most of your experience it's probably worth grabbing a free emergency parachute before strapping yourself in. Otherwise the emphasis will be less on the 'free' and more on the 'falling'. And then, after you've jumped, as you see the ground looming below you, a click of the mouse will deploy

your chute and bring you floating back down to earth with a gentle bump.

Got the hang of it? Good, then it's time to get adventurous. The sky shop offers a wide range of skyboards (including our favourite – a lovely shiny metallic blue one) that make possible all manner of aerobatics, including back flips and cool high-speed dives. Just be sure and keep an eye on the location finder (or better still, get yourself an altimeter for a few hundred Linden dollars) to make sure you don't plummet into the ground at 200 miles an hour – or end up three sims away from where you started.

Skydiving is great fun, but if you want all of the fun of the air without any of the danger, Abbotts also offers a range of

helicopter- and plane tours, as well as flying lessons and charter flights to other parts of the Grid.

And the fun needn't stop there. For Residents who have truly been bitten by the flying bug, and who have a few thousand Linden dollars burning a hole in their cyberpockets, there's nothing cooler than shelling out on a plane of your own. A range of models is on offer, starting from L$700 or so, and while they'll take a bit of getting used to, it's hard to think of a better status symbol to prove that you've truly arrived in Second Life.

Hollywood/Holly Kai One

Hollywood – hooray for it, particularly if you're a fan of yachting or golfing. The first thing you'll notice when you teleport in to virtual Tinsel Town is the attention to detail, right down to the mini-version of the famous Hollywood sign, up on the hills. This must be the place!

The next things you'll notice are the yachts – lots and lots of yachts. Hollywood is the place to come to in Second Life if you want to sail, with lessons available from Starboards yacht club. No matter whether you're an amateur or a salty in-world sea dog, there's a lesson here to fit your needs.

But if yachting's not your bag, the neighbouring Holly Kai

golf club is home to Second Life's largest golf course, playing host to all manner of tournaments and individual games. Prices start at L$150 for half an hour on the driving range and although the experience isn't quite as good as real golf, it's certainly up there with the current crop of virtual golf games – with the added bonus that here you can dress up as Superman and play eighteen holes with your friend, who is dressed like a dragon. Try doing that at St Andrews. (Actually, do. It'd be hilarious.)

For more information on golf in Second Life, visit: **http:// secondlifegolf.wordpress.com/about/**.

Numbakulla

Sporting one of the finest place names on Second Life, Numbakulla is a free adventure game, packed full of puzzles and riddles and with prizes for everyone who completes it. On arriving at Numbakulla you're asked – very politely – to remove any tools or add-ons you might be carrying that could help you cheat, and you're given a notebook to enter clues and other bits of useful information. Then it's time to get stuck in – either on your own or as a part of a small group of puzzle solvers. Extremely clever, extremely addictive.

Tringo

Derived from the words Tetris and Bingo, Tringo is a hybrid game created and played within Second Life. Played with large numbers of players at the same time, Tringo starts with each player being given a 5 x 5 grid, 'printed' on a 'card'. Every few seconds the game shows a new shape which the player has to fit in to the grid. The winner is the first player to fill their grid without leaving any gaps or overlap. Tringo!

Tringo is available in many of Second Life's casinos (see 'After Dark', p. 212) but its home location in-world is in Jarawa.

Nakiska

Home to the Nakiska Ski Club, Nakiska is one of the foremost areas in Second Life for slalom and downhill racing. There are regular organized competitions (look out for notices around the sim) and shops to sell you all the equipment you need, from a bobble hat to a set of super shiny racing skis. In fact the only thing not for sale is a sense of balance – which is something you'll definitely need. And then, when you're done with the slopes, head back to the clubhouse for a drink at the bar or a dip in the roof-top hot tub with your fellow skiers.

SL International Dragstrip

Varooom! Is there anything more exciting than accelerating from nought to sixty faster than a virtual rocket, while strapped into a virtual car, hurtling down a virtual drag strip? Yes, quite a few things actually – but it's still great fun. You don't even need to have your own car as the strip has a healthy stock of them to loan to newbies (see Motorati in the 'Entertainment' chapter (p. 143) for more high-speed action).

Kickboxing at Icedragon's Playpen

Can there be any more relaxing way to spend an afternoon than watching two grown men (or women, or men dressed in rabbit costumes) kicking ten shades of hell out of each other? No, there most certainly cannot. And so praise be for Icedragon's Playpen, where weekly bouts whip Residents into a mad violent frenzy that – one hopes – might at any moment spill out into the streets of Second Life. If you fancy trying your hand at kicking, special equipment is available from the venue and kickboxing pros like Derrick Cult are on hand to show you the ropes.

Babcock Downs

Even the sport of kings is well represented in Second Life, with Muffy Babcock's Babcock Downs providing everything you need to enjoy a day at the races. If gambling is your thing then you can back a favourite – betting actual Linden dollars based on detailed information available for each of the two hundred (and counting) horses stabled at the course. And then, after you've lost your shirt, make sure you save a bit of time to ride the wooden horses on the carousel. Giddy up!

Samurai Island

If you prefer your violent sport with weapons, then Samurai Island is the place for you. Operated by former (real-world) 'exotic dancer' KatanaBlade Anubis, the island is part explorable sim and part combat game, with pitched sword battles the order of the day. The island has hundreds of regular players, and once you enter the game portion, it's all taken very seriously – with numerous competing 'dojos' all trying to be the most handy with a piece of sharpened steel. Watch out for ninjas. They creep up on ya.

Hearts Enchanted

From the vicious to the sublime, Hearts Enchanted is home to the Neo Realms Fishing Camp, an incredibly advanced fishing experience that requires many of the same skills as real-world fishing. Mainly patience and a good strong rod. Fortunately, if you provide the patience then Neo Realms will (for a price) provide the rod, and the bait, and lots and lots of advice. Oh, and as a nice additional touch you can even keep the fish you catch – either to, well, just have or to add to an aquarium if you decide to buy a home in-world (see Going Native, p. 188).

For more Neo Realms camps: **http://fish.neorealms.com**.

Chapter Six:
Shopping and Commerce

As it has developed, one of the most commonly heard criticisms of Second Life concerns its increasing commercialization.

Essentially, there are two types of Second Lifers: those who like to explore and play and don't expect anything in return but the pleasure of entertainment; and those who are there to make money.

Over the last year, Second Life has found itself the centre of increasingly frequent news stories. More often than not, the reason for the story has been connected with money. And naturally, as more money is made in-world, more Real Life corporations and business concerns are eager to get involved and stake their own claims to the thriving metaverse economy.

Whether you see all this commerce as a rapacious cancer turning a decent game – the original point of which was to avoid the whole capitalistic migraine of Real Life – into a kind of MySpace for corporations, or a damn good opportunity, it doesn't alter the fact that money is a significant part of the Second Life experience.

Also, it's worth pointing out that with a particularly talented and virtual world-savvy bunch of companies developing many of the big corporations' sites, the finished result has tended to be pleasantly surprising. In the majority of cases, Second Life business concerns exist in-world for the simple reason that they want to take advantage of what they see as fantastic marketing opportunities, so it's refreshing that the finished results have proved, in many cases, to be highly innovative and surprisingly fun. With synthetic-world experts helming their campaigns, Real Life companies are so far adapting rather well to what is after all an entirely new medium.

In this section, we'll be taking a look at some of the businesses that have set up synthetic shop, and we'll be doing a fair bit of synthetic shopping of our own. Ker-ching!

The Big Three Part I – Rivers Run Red

Avalon – the island formerly known as 'Island' – provided a turning point in many Residents' perspectives on commerce within Second Life. Avalon was one of the first entire islands to be put up to public auction for US dollars at the beginning of 2004, allowing the highest bidder sole renting rights and ultimate power to do whatever they desired with the place.

That highest bidder, Fizik Baskerville of Rivers Run Red fame, made an appearance on the Second Life forums the day after his auction victory and announced to his fellow Residents: 'We are a London- and Chicago-based innovation and branding agency.' Already, alarm bells were beginning to sound. We? Branding agency? What was going on?

'We are commercial-based, but we are fans and active participants,' he continued. 'We will be supporting a charity and promoting good causes. We will need help.' Despite the fine talk and good intentions, there was something in both Baskerville's tone and procedure which was new to the metaverse. It was brazenly corporate.

Residents felt angered and threatened. Firstly, because they were being pushed out of the healthy competition for land and opportunity by wealthy corporations. Secondly because Second Life was being exploited as a marketing tool by companies keen to bring the trendiness and techno-kudos of the metaverse to their own products and promotions. There was a very definite sense of 'they come in here, with their resources and their contacts, buying up our land, building with our prims, eyeing up our virtual wives'. Residents didn't like it, but they must have known they were going to have to lump it.

In a later conversation with James Wagner Au, Baskerville maintained, 'I am not here for confrontation. To me this is an artistic outlet with friends. We are friendly people. Who just wanted a city . . . I have no interest here commercially.' Although a lot of what Avalon has been up to in the last couple of years has borne out much of what Baskerville was saying in the early days about community, art, and creativity

– see the film festivals, the music festivals, the exhibitions – that last remark clearly isn't quite true.

So far, Rivers Run Red can count amongst their clients Duran Duran, who are currently promising to play a concert in Avalon; Penguin Books, with whom they collaborated on the in-world promotion of *Snow Crash*; 20th Century Fox, with whom they premiered *X Men 3*; Disney, with whom they've worked extensively to replicate content of *The Hitchhiker's Guide to the Galaxy*, the *Pirates of the Caribbean* sequels and *The Chronicles of Narnia*; the BBC, with whom they staged Radio 1's Big Weekend Virtual Festival; and so on.

There can be little doubt that the majority of the projects they are becoming involved with are creative and innovative, but let's face it: they also sell shoes . . .

Adidas

At the 2006 Second Life Community Convention, Rivers Run Red announced that they would be creating a virtual presence for sneaker super-merger Adidas Reebok. In reality, or indeed virtual reality, there is only so much you can do with a pair of trainers. To their credit, together with their digital gurus, Adidas haven't done too bad a job, but still, it's just footwear.

The Adidas store is located in Adidas (appropriately enough) and on first sight, it's impressive only because it looks like one of those ultra-modern, metallic, and clinical stores you see in Real Life. Except with giant astronauts hovering about the place telling you how to buy Adidas a3 Microrides – for that is the shoe that Adidas is flogging in-world at L$50 a pair. The trainer, boast the info cards around their plot, 'comes in two colourways, black and orange (High Jumper) or white and blue (Astronaut).' Colourways? Whatever. What's nice about the Adidas store and promotion is that you can test the shoes out if you're unsure how your pixellated alter ego might feel in them. There are special test mats either side of the store on which you can try out the high-jumping features (High Jumper) or the 'float' (Astronaut). Somewhat less palatable is the suspicion that, sometime soon, every other person in the metaverse will be bouncing past you in exactly the same, increasingly annoying 'colourways'.

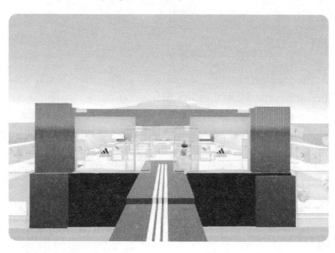

What's great about Second Life is the individuality that so many designers and builders bring to the party. Adidas and others are in a sense threatening to stand in the way of that creativity, threatening to homogenize Second Life. Of course it could be argued that all Adidas are actually doing is catering to a demand that already exists. If people didn't want to buy their trainers (in either Lives), then they wouldn't. And if creative independents stop creating merely because some of their customers are going the corporate route, then their hearts were probably never really in it anyway. It is, after all, a business. If they're in it for the pleasure of creating, then they'll go on doing so with or without any commercial success.

All fair enough.

But a lot of people like Second Life because it's somewhere they can get away from all the insincerity, the homogeneity, the brashness of capitalism. Or rather it used to be.

IBM

In September 2006, at the end of what it called an online 'innovation jam' – or a meeting to discuss new initiatives – IBM announced that it was to spend $100 million on new projects, many of which would involve developing and manufacturing the soft- and hardware to power virtual 3D worlds. In October CEO Edward Palmisano was featured in *Business Week* boasting about the two avatars he had running around in Second Life. One was a rather strait-laced Palmisano, one imagines closely related to the man himself as he goes about his everyday business, the other a less-controlled anything-goes kind of guy. A CEO who lets his hair down.

At the time of writing, the IBM island, Hursley, is being kept strictly under wraps, so we'll have to wait and see what IBM has in mind for its vast virtual market.

Incidentally, the vast majority of groups in Second Life are free to join. Because it's not about money – it's about community. IBM Employees Worldwide, however, costs a Linden tenner. Make of that what you will.

The History of Second Life, Part Three: The Second Life Boston Tea Party

The more you discover about Second Life, the more you will tend to agree that it's not just a game, from the simple fact that everything within it is created by the Residents them-selves, to the fact that even the most intrinsic rules or laws of this virtual society are – when the people decree it so – open to change.

But then, take another look – there are little people run-ning around with wings and dogs' penises: of course it's a bloody game. On the other hand, whoever heard of a game in which you pay tax?

What happened during the Tax Revolt in the latter half of 2003 has all the hallmarks of game-playing, albeit somewhat chaotic and surreal game-playing, but of course at heart the tax revolt was very, very serious, because it was to do with real money.

At this point in Second Life's evolution, Residents were charged tax to build property. This was tax in Linden dollars payable to Linden Lab. The tax system, however, was unfairly weighted against more ambitious Residents. Which is to say that Residents who built skyscrapers or football stadiums would be charged a much higher rate than those who stuck to very basic projects. Understandably these Residents felt that they were being penalized for making Second Life more enjoyable for others and so they began to protest.

At the time there existed in Second Life a place called Americana. Americana was, as the name suggests, a space in which users recreated great American icons: the Statue of Liberty, the Washington Monument, Route 66, and so on. Awash with grand designs, Americana was the obvious choice for this particular protest. By early August, grumbling had turned to action and the Washington Memorial had been replaced with an enormous stack of tea crates. Protesters wore T-shirts which read 'Born Free – Taxed To Death'. Billboards sprang up declaring 'Don't Tread On Me'. And an angry midget set fire to a petrol station on Route 66.

Leading the revolt was a catwoman named Fleabite Beach. Approached by Wagner James Au for *New World Notes*, Beach laid out the protesters' manifesto, a modern-day

Declaration of Independence for a modern-day virtual world.

As protests began to spread throughout the rest of the world, with tea crates popping up all over the place, Fleabite Beach made the promise that if the complaints of the people were not heeded, 'we shall make of ourselves soldiers of the heart, embracing Liberty and Justice for all; and rejecting law and dictate made in haste to the detriment of just and free-thinking men, women and cats everywhere. To the Mad Mad King George we shall say, "You and your kind will rue the day. To you, sirs, Tea Crates in the Bay."'

This continued for a couple of months, with further protests, endless meetings, and all the usual playful prankish-ness of online dissent. And in the end, the protesters were successful and the inequities in the tax system were overturned.

Midnight City

Dating back to 2004, Midnight City currently takes the form of an island located in the Umber sim. Founded by one Mistress Midnight, this is, as its name suggests, a tiny city which is renowned in-world for its sterling shopportunities, particularly in the lingerie department, but which also has a residential area, including a slum, as well its own cinema, football pitch, and club. It's also the home of numerous activities, including Trin and Nala's radio show and a rather marvellous vampire role-playing game. Real vampires not allowed.

Midnight City was built by Aimee Weber, who has a flourishing business providing content creation and services to businesses and other organizations looking to work within Second Life. To date, she has collaborated with such diverse entities as the American Cancer Society, the United Nations, and American Apparel.

Wiccan Shop

If you're a fan of religious or even romantic but slightly pre-tentious rituals, then you can pick up everything you need to make a really top-rank one at the Wiccan Shop in Bbang.

As well as everything you might need for a full-on neo-pagan freakout – your high-quality altar tools, your staffs, your cloaks, your dresses, gloves, and masks; your wands, your pentagrams, your chalices, and athames bowls – you can also pick up more everyday stuff – your candles. And some beautiful ornaments. It also does a nice line in Goddess Wear and meditation, for when you want to look, and feel, that extra bit special.

The Big Three Part II – The Electric Sheep Company

Second of the Big Three Second Life development companies is the Electric Sheep Company. According to its website, Electric Sheep 'offers solutions for virtual world commerce, creativity and community'.

Thus far, the ESC has perhaps the coolest portfolio of collaborators and projects, as well as what is probably the most prolific output. The company designed and built Reuters Island, with the Reuters HUD which pulls live news headlines into various locations; developed Sony BMG's space on Media Island, with its Christina Aguilera and DMX fan rooms and of course the aloft hotel, which staged the Ben Folds performance that realized instant in-world legendary status (see over); collaborated with Major League Baseball to bring the Home Run Derby and live baseball to Second Life, the latter featuring real players replaced by dinky little 'bobbleheads' playing out the live action on the field; at the behest of MTV, built a replica of Laguna Beach that now features the popular nudist area, which is a wonderful place to go and let it all hang out, especially, it seems, if you are a man desperate to show off your new genitals; brought the first museum exhibition into Second Life, a collaboration with George Eastman House and the National Meteorological Center (for whom it also built their own museum, library, and campus, complete with gondola ride); with Lego, built the live Mindstorms

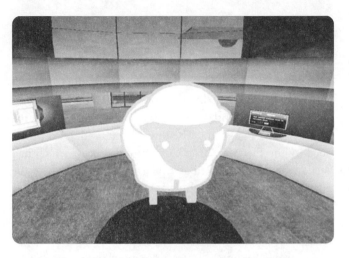

event, which allowed Residents to have a go at building their own robots; and constructed a floating island for the Text 100 PR company, which features free assisted flying packs and handy tips on writing a press release. Just in case that's your bag.

ESC has also built machinima sets for *CBS News* and the BBC's *Newsnight*, as well as a spectacular 3D Art Room, bringing to life some of the greats of twentieth-century Modernism.

And that really is just scratching the surface.

aloft island

The day after Second Life hit the one million Resident mark in October 2006, Starwood Hotels held the official launch party of its new in-world hotel, the virtual aloft hotel (with deliberate, and doubtless very trendy, lower-case 'a'), on the Sony BMG Media Island. The three-month build was developed by the Electric Sheep Company, a process which had been meticulously tracked on a blog specifically set up for the purpose. The party also doubled as a publicity event for a new album. Ben Folds played live. Residents who wanted to attend were asked to email the hotel and book a VIP ticket. The launch was overbooked.

According to some sources, the concert did not go exactly as planned and resulted in the following headline in the *Second Life Herald*: 'Washed-up Emo Musician Drops F-Bomb on Fans in SL'. The 'F-Bomb' occurred when Ben Folds was asked why his song 'Rent-a-cop' was on the new album. Ben Folds' response kicked off with a rather surly 'Fuck you'. The *Herald* wasn't impressed. Many of Folds' fans, however – who perhaps knew more of what to expect from Folds, who by the way was never Emo – had a whale of a time. How many other gigs can you go to, they rightly wondered, where the performer gets drunk on Duff beer, fires lasers from his eyes, challenges the audience with a light sabre, then slays one of them? Not that many, surely.

But back to the hotel. The aloft hotel is actually a virtual version of a new hotel Starwood plans to launch in Real Life in 2008. However contemptuous some people may be about the exponential commercialization of Second Life, no one can deny that the aloft hotel is a brilliant marketing device. And even if the pool is only a synthetic one, the water looks lovely.

Free Stuff

Thankfully not everything is Second Life is obtainable only through the power of the Linden dollar. There is also a great deal of free stuff out there too. In fact there is free stuff just about everywhere. Clicking on boxes and balls all over Second Life can yield some surprisingly nifty freebies.

A couple of great places for newbies keen to bulk out their wardrobe arc Free Dove and the Freebie Warehouse. Both are awash with just about any item of clothing or accessory you can imagine. They're not quite up there in terms of style or, obviously, exclusivity as the stuff you have to fork out for, but if you're not enormously fashion-conscious but balk at the idea of wearing the same clothes two days in a row, then these are the places to come.

Luskwood Creatures

In Second Life, you never have to look the same from one day to the next. Not only can you change your appearance as subtly or as drastically as you can imagine using the regular body-sculpting tools, but if you want a complete change, all you have to do is buy yourself a new avatar. You can buy as many as you like, in fact, and when the mood takes you, slip one out of your inventory and become someone, or indeed something, else entirely. Avatars of infinite variety are available throughout the known metaverse, but if it's furries you're after, you can't go wrong with the legendary Luskwood Creatures.

Luskwood Creatures are credited as builders of some of the first anthropomorphic avatars in Second Life. Here at their furry paradise bodymall, why not take the humanity off your feet and set yourself up as a rakish squirrel or a fwuffy wabbit. Alternatively, you could go to the dark side of furry with a (still awfully cute) fox, wolf, or even dragon. Do what you like. It's your Second Life. Go on. At least try one on. You might actually feel more comfortable with fur.

They even do a bit of charity work both out- and in-world, auctioning off limited-edition avatars. But they don't like to bark about it.

A Source of Talent

As well as thousands of Residents shopping for shows and sex toys at any one time, Second Life also has its fair share of talent-spotters out there. The amount of creation and innovation that goes into a great many of Second Life's synthetic artefacts is staggering. The metaverse has become a hive for some of Real Life's most talented, most committed, and, perhaps more importantly, most instinctive programmers, engineers, and artists. Before starting work on its own 3D intranet, IBM was reported to have paid one of its software engineers to experience Second Life first. Meanwhile a London-based agency, Greene & Heaton, which represents such literary luminaries as P. D. James and Michael Frayn, became in October 2006 the first to move in-world. As well as taking advantage of the still relatively novel concept of having a virtual office, Greene & Heaton hope to snag a bestseller in one of the many writers' groups that have sprung up in Second Life.

Dell Island

At the end of November 2006, Dell arrived in Second Life with Dell Island. On its website, the company explains how Michael Dell started building and selling personal computers from stock parts when he was at university and that what began as a hobby developed into the huge corporation we know today. Innovation has always been at the heart of Dell, it tells us. Also important to Dell, apparently, is 'the idea of working directly with its customers', which is what has brought it to Second Life. At the time of writing, Dell Island is 'far from finished', so we hope that by the time you're reading this, Dell has built a virtual call centre, preferably on another sim in a completely different part of the world, where its staff can continue the company's proud history of working directly with its customers.

Dell kicked off its presence in Second Life with a press conference, attended by the ubiquitous Philip Linden (that is, Second Life's founder Philip Rosedale.). A free computer was offered to the first person to buy a system in-world. It's also offering oh-so-trendy Dell-branded merchandise such as backpacks and T-shirts, as well of course as customer support and sales. Customers can pop along to the Dell factory and see 3D interactive views of products they might wish to buy. And for the real Dell enthusiast, there's even a museum. What more could you want? Go on. Go to Dell.

Aimee Weber

Another emerging star in the world of Second Life site development is Aimee Weber. Offering everything that any company might need to establish a virtual presence in the metaverse, Weber, according to her own website, 'has been recognized as one of the best in Second Life for architecture, texturing, fashion design, project management, and virtual marketing'.

So far, Weber's most famous, or at least most frequently cited, collaborations have been with American Apparel, the giant US leotard and pant emporium, and the Midnight City complex. But she has also been involved with other much more interesting projects. As well as project-managing the American Cancer Society's virtual Relay For Life in July 2006, Weber was also responsible for the United Nations Stand Up Against Poverty event, which featured a concert by the rock band Sugarcult, who performed for free in support.

Weber is also heavily involved in various educational projects, including work with the National Oceanic and

Atmospheric Administration and the Earth System Research Laboratory. With these organizations Weber has developed fully interactive educational demonstrations concerning the oceans, the climate, and anything and everything else regarding gigantic masses of air and water. Other features include a real-time melting glacier, a submarine ride, a tsunami, and an aeroplane ride into a hurricane. She also worked with the Exploratorium Museum on various events to coincide with the solar eclipse in Turkey in March 2006. On a similar theme, her in-world Tour of the Solar System should not be missed.

Aimee Weber's trademarks are the vibrancy, light, and colour of her designs. Her American Apparel build was the first structure in Second Life to reflect the changing light of different times of day. During daylight hours, the building

The Regina Spektor Audio Kiosk

reflects the sunlight, whereas at night it is swathed in spot-lights and interior lighting seeping out into the darkness.

Our personal favourite Aimee Weber work to date is her collaboration with Warner Brothers Records on the Regina Spektor Audio Kiosk. This is basically a trendy New York loft apartment in Slackstreet where you can kick back and chill out to Spektor's music. Or if that gets too much for you, you can nip up the iron staircase and have a snooze.

The Big Three Part III – Millions of Us

Millions of Us is another branding and advertising agency, focused on bringing real-world companies into virtual worlds. It was founded by Reuben Steiger, who previously ran business development for Linden Lab, attempting to convince the outside world that Second Life was the next generation of the Internet.

Amongst its projects so far, Millions of Us brought Jay-Z to Second Life – or at least, his avatar – in a mixed-reality performance which was shown in-world as well as on ABC's show *Jimmy Kimmel Live*; organized the in-world launch of *Popular Science Magazine*; built Scion City for Toyota, a site described by Steiger as 'a huge, futuristic, decaying twilight city, amazingly lit and a great place to drive'; created the head-quarters for *Wired* magazine, with the office layout built to resemble a giant circuit board; and collaborated with General Motors on the build of Motorati, the Pontiac project described as an auto-civilization. Millions of Us has also worked with Sun Microsystems, Intel, and Fox Atomic Studios, amongst others.

Toyota

There are places in Second Life which really sing out to the imagination. Sights and sounds which stagger you, baffle you, or make you laugh. Out loud. Places where everything you see and click on will do something you didn't expect. Places like the Crooked House, Warren Ellis' Integral Bay, and the Lost Gardens of Apollo. Then there's Toyota's virtual showroom, launched in Second Life in August 2006 to promote the exciting new Scion model. Maybe, just maybe, if you're really into Toyotas, you might enjoy taking your time over the posters that ramble on and on about the various specifications and no doubt very exciting possibilities, but you're probably better off going to the website. And maybe the idea of taking a virtual Toyota for a test drive tickles your fancy, but really, at the moment, the technology just isn't good enough. You'd probably be better off playing Rollcage and simply *pretending* you're in a Toyota.

But wait! What's this? Did we speak too soon? It seems we did. Between two of the showroom models a small Perspex lectern reads: 'If you're a Second Life savvy texture artist, builder or scripter, this is likely your perfect car – with full permission to edit most elements, your Scion can be totally unique! Make any change you want . . . give your Scion the full custom paint job of your dreams!' This is actually where Scion City comes into its own and many of the customized, or 'tricked-out', versions of the Scion, as created by Second Life Residents, are worth seeing. At the time of writing, Toyota has yet to decide whether it's going to allow Residents to set up their own dealerships in Scion City. It probably will, of course, as it can only be good for business.

Pontiac (Motorati Island)

Hot on the heels of Toyota (Nissan too, who opened a virtual dealership in October) came General Motors' Pontiac division in November. Presently the only model available in Second Life is the Pontiac Solstice GXP, but more will follow for sure. The dealership is located in Motorati Island, a 96-acre plot which General Motors plans to give away, plot by plot, in land grants to Second Life Residents keen to practise their automobile-building skills. This scheme they have christened Land-a-Palooza. 'Become a partner with Pontiac and create a thriving island of car culture,' its website beckons. 'Let your imagination run wild . . . Consider us insane landlords with a taste for fast cars and big ideas.'

Still under construction at the time of writing, the General Motors plot does have the potential to be more interesting

than your average car dealership, with ideas for future development including drive-in movies, drive-in restaurants, and probably a great many other things, into which you can drive. More on Motorati Island and its famous racetrack in the 'Entertainment' chapter (p. 143).

Sun Microsystems

In October 2006, Sun Microsystems proudly declared itself the first Fortune 500 company to host an event in Second Life. The event was a press conference at which Sun showed off the new in-world pavilion it had just built and spoke of a future where business and virtual worlds might increasingly intermingle. The press conference was chaired by Philip Rosedale, Sun's Chief Researcher, Jon Gage, and its Chief Gaming Officer, Chris Melissinos. Gage explained that every year at their largest developer conference, they get to meet twenty-two thousand developers, whereas in the future, in Second Life, he could meet millions.

We don't really think he's thought it through, though. He could certainly get a much larger number than twenty-two thousand all together on Second Life – at the time of writing, the average amount of people actually online at the same time is generally between ten and fifteen thousand, but that number is spread out across the entire metaverse. So, twenty-two thousand alone would need a damn big build. Millions, however, would pose a serious problem. After all, avatars take up space too.

Meanwhile Melissinos explained that Second Life is not a game. No. 'It's an amazing platform for global communications.' OK, of course he's right. But let's not forget the Furries.

The History of Second Life, Part Four: The Declaration of Independence

After the upheaval of the in-world 'Boston Tea Party', Linden Lab sought the advice of Lawrence Lessig, Stanford law professor, advocate of Creative Commons (see p. 160), and author. Lessig attended a meeting to discuss what could be done about the recent discontent and how things should progress in Second Life in general.

Shortly afterwards, in November 2003, the tax system was abolished and a new policy was introduced which conferred intellectual property rights on all Residents.

According to the Second Life site:

'It's true! Second Life v 1.2 puts an end to the stress and confusion of object and property taxes. Even better, it no longer costs you a single Linden Dollar to build objects in-world. A vastly simplified economy in v 1.2 means that you own what you own and can build as you please – with no worries about a property tax bill hitting you at the end of the week.'

Replacing the tax system was a new land model, which basically allowed Residents to pay monthly rent in US dollars on virtual land. This enabled Residents, and real-world companies and corporations, to hold entire islands in Second Life.

In a nutshell, living and building in Second Life became much more economically viable.

The consequences of this were of course immense, with what can be described as a great scramble for land kicking off in December 2003. Indeed *Wired* magazine equated the rush with the concept of Manifest Destiny within American history, that is, the voracious appetite for expansionism that has so defined America's ideology since the term was coined midway through the nineteenth century.

Within Second Life, then, a period of industry hitherto unknown was embarked upon. Sticking with the American history analogy, we have now moved into the Gilded Age. This culminated in a huge influx of well-established Real Life businesses setting up shop in Second Life. At the time of writing, IBM, MTV, Microsoft, the BBC, Reuters, Coca Cola, and many, many more have established a presence in Second Life. Although there is no doubt that the popularity of Second Life has increased as a consequence, there is also a great deal of frustration that corporations have wandered in with the sole intention of exploiting Second Life as a marketing tool for their products. Many Residents are of the opinion that the commercialization of Second Life is ruining it. But then, many residents of the real world feel exactly the same.

That's capitalism for you.

From which point, Second Life has gone from strength to strength. Membership fees were reduced at the same time as tax was abolished, but in September 2005, free membership was introduced. At that stage, there were 45,000 Residents. Just over a year later, on 18 October 2006, the population hit 1,000,000. Within two weeks of that, a further 200,000 had signed up.

Xcite

Once you've experienced a certain amount of intimacy in Second Life, you may suddenly get the urge to buy yourself some genitals. No one in Second Life comes equipped with genitals. Nor do they grow over time. Rather, like a frustrated little Action Man or Barbie, you have to shuffle into a shop that specializes in such things. Thankfully, there are many such places in Second Life. The place with the most extensive range, however, has got to be Xcite.

Xcite is an adult-entertainment shopping bonanza. If it concerns the sexual peccadilloes of your avatar and you can't get it at Xcite, then it probably hasn't been invented yet. Javier

Puff joined Second Life in July 2005. He went through the whole process of settling into his new skin and acclimatizing to his new world, then someone gave him some old genitals they weren't using. Javier wasn't impressed, and so he set about making his own. And that was that. Word of Javier's hot new privates spread like wildfire and everybody wanted a piece of him. Within a couple of months, Xcite was born.

At first, of course, trade was mainly restricted to penises and vaginas, but before very long Xcite was branching out into nipples, rear ends, and . . . well, you name it. A quick wander around Xcite and you can fill your basket, not to mention your boots, with all manner of kinky paraphernalia. Everything from whips, handcuffs, pasties, gags, floggers, balls and chains and collars and leads to piercings, pose balls, blindfolds, riding crops, cattle prods, spiked paddles, and furniture. You know the kind of furniture we mean.

It is a bizarre experience trawling round a place like Xcite, eyeing up genitals, trying to pick out a penis that might suit you. Or maybe picking out a nice vagina for your wife.

For all of its sex, Xcite manages to come across – ahem – as quite a restrained – ahem – and almost tasteful environment. None of the in-your-face bukkake mayhem of certain other places we stumbled across in our search for synthetic masculation.

In short, if it's virtual sex you're after, Xcite is the virtual sex palace for you.

Charity

Just because something has to do with commerce doesn't mean it's necessarily a money-grabbing corporation lining its own corporate pockets at the expense of the little people. An increasing number of charities are making themselves visible in-world, taking advantage of Second Life's surging popularity and hoping to siphon off a few extra Linden dollars for their good causes.

As well as official charity efforts, more and more Second Lifers are hosting their own charity events. Many artists have made works available for sale in in-world galleries with proceeds going to good causes. And in 2006, a group of Residents staged a U2 tribute concert in Second Life, complete with Bono and the Edge avatars and a streamed recording of a real U2 gig. The gig was free, and not authorized by the band, but was put on to raise awareness of U2's charitable donations to Make Poverty History. And raise awareness it certainly did, with reports of the gig appearing around the (real) world. The gig itself is long finished but several videos of the event are available to view via **http://www.youtube.com**. Popular Second Life Charity activities include . . .

The Second Life Relay For Life

Hosted annually, the Second Life Relay For Life for the American Cancer Society has already become one of the biggest events on the in-world calendar. Each year some of

Second Life's most capable designers collaborate to map out a course for avatars to walk through, making charitable donations as they go. The course changes every year but in 2006 it included a stroll through a virtual representation of London – featuring the London Eye – as well as taking in Paris, where one enterprising Resident organized base jumps off the Eiffel Tower. To find out about the next event see **http://www.can cer.org**.

The Save the Children Yak Shack

The Save the Children Fund was the first UK-based charity to open for business in Second Life, and the Save the Children Yak Shack build was the first to sell yaks. The Yak Shack allows Residents to pay L$1,000 for a virtual beast which they are

then able to customize to their heart's content. The Yak Shack also provides access to information about the Save the Children Fund as well as other ways to raise money for the organization. And did we mention the yaks?

The World Development Movement

Another UK charity, the World Development Movement, claims to be the first to have opened a permanent base of operations in-world. There's plenty of information about the group and how to give, but the centrepiece of the WDM area is a giant poverty-death counter that shows the number of children who have died from poverty since Second Life was founded. A number of Second Lifers have expressed concern that the counter is somehow out of place in Second Life and that it is somehow implying that the in-world community is not doing enough to help, rather than encouraging it to do more. Whatever your view, the death counter is a striking reminder of the world outside Second Life and a brilliant way to raise awareness of one of the smaller charities.

Keep an eye on **http://secondlife.com/events** for upcoming charity events.

Chapter Seven:
Entertainment

Of all the real-world companies that have established in-world outposts, it's the entertainment organizations that are really leading the pack. Both international entertainment giants such as Sony BMG and public-service broadcasters like the BBC have set up shop in-world, with Sony hosting live gigs and the BBC even broadcasting an edition of its current-affairs programme *Newsnight* in-world. But it's not just the big boys – there are hundreds of independent nightclubs, bars, and venues represented online, many of which are well worth spending an hour or so in. But where to start . . . ?

Live Venues

Media Island

As we've already mentioned, the Electric Sheep Company is the design company responsible for many of Second Life's coolest developments (p. 120). One such, Media Island, is the home of music and entertainment company Sony BMG.

As the main complex rezzes in front of your eyes, you

could be forgiven for thinking you've taken a wrong turning and ended up at Stansted Airport in England – but no, it's definitely Sony. You can tell by the huge amount of advertising. Look! There's an advert for Christina Aguilera! Look! There's Alice in Chains! Clicking on a useful teleport board allows you to jump to the various areas – the artists' lounge, the legacy artists' lounge (like the artists' lounge, one assumes, but with a stair-lift), and the loft, which plays host to all manner of live gigs and events.

Motorati – the Fairgrounds Raceway

Motorati is the home of Pontiac on Second Life and so as you'd expect it's chock-full of cars and car-related things. Naturally there are plenty of cars to buy, starting at around L$600, and if you're in a speedy mood, the Fairgrounds Raceway is among the most exciting race tracks in-world, not least because it was built by a female hyena called Suki Ming. Fairgrounds offers two ways to get involved: either casually (just turn up with a car or bike and burn rubber) or officially (Thursday night is race night, with prizes on offer for the brightest and best Second Life racers).

But the reason Motorati belongs in the entertainment category is because alongside all the cars, it's also a major entertainment venue, thanks to a dedicated music stage. Previous gigs include a Jay-Z show simultaneously broadcast in Motorati and in Hollywood Boulevard in the real world, with lots more events promised.

Muse Isle

Muse Isle describes itself as a 'place for those who make art and those who enjoy art to come together in a way that isn't possible or practical in the real world'. The main music space on Muse Isle is the Muse Arena, an incredible piece of construction, not unlike a Roman amphitheatre, albeit with slightly more contemporary entertainment, and fewer lions. The island has a frequently updated list of forthcoming live events at **http://www.muse-isle.com** – otherwise you can just drop by any time to meet your fellow music lovers and wait for someone to take to the stage and start strumming.

Old Salt's Pub

As one of Second Life's most established music pubs, Old Salt's is a great place to hear the bands that other Residents are talking about. And of course, being a pub, there's no shortage of conversation and drink too. The Old Salt's website – **http://www.oldsaltspub.com** – has details of all the upcoming events as well as profiles of the pub's regular performers including Silas Scarborough, Dallas Horsefly, and folk singer Push Chandler.

The Three Lions/Bourton Village

Proof that Americans don't have the monopoly on hostelries in Second Life, the Three Lions is a traditional English local boozer complete with beer-stained carpets and a dartboard.

With a decent crowd of regulars – and some deeply cheesy eighties music – you could be forgiven for thinking you're holed up in a pub in any English village. But this isn't any village – this is Bourton, one of the few totally uncommercial villages in-world. All the entertainment is free, there's no trading allowed, and you can't buy or rent property. What you can do, however, is bounce on the Union Jack bouncy castle and swim in the paddling pool full of melted Toblerone.

The Hummingbird Café

If you prefer your music accompanied by a bite to eat rather than booze, then the Hummingbird Café is happy to oblige. Like Old Salt's Pub the emphasis here is on an intimate venue, with up-close live (frequently acoustic) music. No hummingbirds, though, which is a disappointment.

Second Life Music (Official)

Not a venue, but an information source, the official Second Life Music site at **http://secondlife.com/community/music.php** has up-to-the-minute listings of live music events in-world. From intimate gigs by new artists up to huge outdoor festivals starring the biggest artists from the real world, this is the place to find out who's on, where.

Festivals

BBC Radio 1/One Big Weekend

The UK's public-service broadcaster has been no slouch when it comes to adopting new technologies, and its approach to Second Life is no different. Although at the time of writing the BBC Radio 1 virtual stage is lying empty, the venue has been specially designed to host live concerts all year round. The first event was a virtual version of the station's 'One Big Weekend' event, hosted in Second Life at the same time as the real event in Dundee. Featuring acts such as Razorlight and Muse, the event also allowed Residents to pick up free Radio 1 radios and headphones so they could enjoy the music as they wandered around in-world. Whatever will they think of next?

Burning Life

Another festival that exists both in-world and in the real world, Burning Man is an annual event held in Nevada's Black Rock desert. Famous for its artistic attendees, its lax attitude to public nudity, and its climax – the burning of a gigantic wooden man – it's exactly the kind of event that would be right at home in Second Life. And so it is. But if you're planning to pay a visit to the annual Burning Life event, you'll have to get your timing right – the event's location is subject to change and like the real-world event, it only lasts for one week of the year (ending on America's Labor Day), after which the whole thing is dismantled until the next year.

Nightclubs and Bars

We'll deal with the seedier side of Second Life nightlife in the 'After Dark' chapter (p. 204), but in the meantime, there are plenty of places to go if you fancy a drink and a dance and – of course – a chance to meet the opposite sex.

One of the cleverest things about Second Life is the fact that you are able to listen to streamed music whenever you enter buildings or regions. This ingenious use of technology means that nightclubs and bars are able to offer real-life DJs to entertain you as you dance. And dance you can, thanks to Second Life's animation features – just have a root around your inventory, double-click on one of the pre-installed dance moves, and get partying. Or if you're feeling adventurous, many clubs allow you to download new moves suited to their music – from hard rock to waltz to Russian Cossack dancing.

The Shelter In Exile

One of the first non-sex-themed clubs in Second Life, the Shelter claims to be one of the friendliest nightspots in-world. In fact it's not really a nightclub at all – more a help

The Shelter in Exile

spot for newbies that happens to play music. Everyone is welcome, not just the young 'uns, and the mass-appeal music policy reflects that (although quite who 'Turning Japanese' by the Vapors is aimed at is unclear). The venue also hosts weekly live gigs which are usually well attended by a good cross-section of Residents. If you're looking to hook up with a new partner, this is probably the wrong place to hang out, but if you fancy a middle-of-the-road drink, a chance to meet new friends, and even a little help finding your way around Second Life, you won't find better.

The Dive

For those of you who like your Scotch with a little bit of water, you could do worse than the Dive; surely the world's first undersea nightclub, where revellers dance amongst 'live' sharks and crabs and new dance moves are downloaded by clicking on a giant mermaid. To get into the club, simply tele-port – or fly – to the club's above-ground decking and take a walk over the side into the water. No jeans, no trainers, no flippers. Also, you'll be hard pushed to find a friendlier bar owner than the Dive's Wolfgang Fonck. Even better, Dive staff member Sierra Sugar doesn't need much persuading to take dance-weary revellers for a relaxing metaverse tour in her wonderful hot-air balloon. Hopefully, by the time you get round to it, she will have learned to fly the thing properly.

Rockers' Requiem

Rockers' Requiem is a rock-themed club (or more accurately a metal-, rock-, goth-, and punk-themed club) – and is possi-bly the oldest venue of its type in Second Life. Situated in Mieto, the club boasts genuinely entertaining DJs and a crowd of regulars who know each other – and the DJs – by name. Imagine a cyber version of Cheers, with neck piercings, and you're pretty much there. If you've got a strong stomach, a visit to the first floor is a must for the 'Gallery of Gore'; otherwise, explore the rest of the building for the biggest mosh pit in-world and a 'strippers' lounge' tucked away in the corner, when you want to kick back and watch someone else do the dancing.

Castle Sable Open Air Ballroom

When is a nightclub not a nightclub? When it's outside, in the daytime, and offers waltzes and tangos. Don't worry if you have two left feet, dancing like a pro is a simple matter of grabbing your partner, clicking on a free dance ball, and sweeping onto the dance floor. And it's all situated in the delightful grounds of Castle Sable. Romantic, romantic, romantic.

Wheelies

Located in Stevensville – Second Life's dedicated disability sim – Wheelie's is the brainchild of Simon Stevens, who suffers from cerebral palsy. And it's a perfect example of why

Second Life is so important. Essentially it's a nightclub specially designed for disabled and able-bodied clubbers to come together and dance the night away. And it has live events and competitions too. Well worth a visit. (Although we would have called it 'Chairs!')

The Lava Pit

Run by the brilliantly named Lord Leafblower and Aava Jeegoo, the Lava Pit is a great place for newbies to find their dancing feet thanks to the club's conveniently situated 'dance mats'. Just step on a mat and with a couple of clicks you'll be dancing smoother than John Travolta. Or possibly Michael Jackson. Whichever you prefer. There's also an arts gallery, a fun park, and a sandpit to play in when you're all danced out.

The Pink Pantheress Lounge

If you like your dance clubs to be pink, then welcome to the pinkest place in the metaverse. Formerly known as the Pink Panther lounge, in homage to the cartoon cat of the same name (who was of course based on the film of the same name), the Pink Pantheress lounge is a truly twenty-four-hour experience with a daily roster of live DJs playing throughout the club. See **http://www.thepinkpantherlounge.com** for the full run-down of who's on when.

Club Industry

An absolutely rammed club playing electro pop, darkwave, synthpop, and all that good stuff. Boasts a truly impressive lighting rig and two stages for live performances. Enough said.

Cinemas and Film

Hollywood Academy of Movies (HAM)

Where else to begin an exploration of Second Life cinema than in Hollywood? Of course we already stopped by Tinsel Town back in the 'Sport, Leisure, and Games' chapter (p. 103), thanks to Second Life Hollywood's magnificent yachting and golfing facilities – but it's cinema where the sim really comes into its own. Even the setting of the Hollywood Academy of Movies is impressive. Based in the Chinese Theatre (Grauman's, in this case), there's even a walk of fame outside, featuring the names of real Oscar winners in gold stars set into the pavement. And around the edges of the path you'll see reproductions of famous movie posters from recent years, including *Titanic* and *Schindler's List*.

On stepping across HAM's threshold, the first thing you'll see is a gaggle of 'lifesized' cut-outs of film stars – from Marilyn Monroe to the chap in the red suit from *The Incredibles* – which, it has to be said, lend a tacky air to the proceedings. But not as tacky as Hollywood Apparel, the gift shop selling such treats as a *Casablanca* 'experience' gift plate, whatever one of those is. Presumably you'd use it to serve a hill of beans.

Fortunately, things improve when you step inside the main building, with all sorts of treats to amuse the film buff – from votes for the best movie of all time to the Hall of Fame on the second floor featuring legends from every era of cinema. In fact the only thing missing was any actual film to watch – an odd oversight for a place that calls itself a 'theatre'.

Machinima: Second Life's burgeoning movie industry

Like all unique cultures, there exists a thriving film industry within Second Life. And where most real-world cultures use real people as actors, it seems only appropriate that the players in Second Life movieland are avatars themselves. Machinima is a curious sub-set of animation where scenes are acted out by players in either traditional computer games, or in online game/virtual world environments. These scenes are recorded and edited into actual films. The versatility of Second Life makes it the perfect location to film machinima.

Leading the way in Second Life machinima is a group who call themselves alt-zoom (**http://www.alt-zoom.com**). The group host regular film festivals where members are encouraged to record their own films in-world, usually on a set theme. Previous themes include the Ed Wood Machinima Festival ('No Time, No Budget, No Good'), based on the work of the famous so-bad-he-was-good filmmaker, with prizes totalling L\$60,000 in categories like Worst Film, Worst Story, Worst Acting, Worst Costumes, and Most Disturbing Film (see **http://alt-zoom.com/edwood.htm** for more).

More information about Second Life machinima can be found at **http://secondlife.com/showcase/machinima.php** – or by searching for 'Second Life machinima' on Youtube. com.

A great example of the genre, *Bells and Spurs*, filmed entirely in-world, can be found at **http://bellsandspurs.com**.

Natural Selection Studios

Natural Selection studios is a dedicated film studio, based in-world. Originally established to film Second Life weddings (see 'Going Native' (p. 200) for more on these curious ceremonies), the company soon decided that its creative ambitions went beyond nuptials and began creating 'presentations for both education and marketing'. Natural Selection's headquarters is a funny-looking beast with lots of sharp edges and floating goldfish and waterfalls pouring out of walls. But there's also a big viewing screen at the front, showing the company's latest features to an appreciative audience.

Laguna Beach

Produced in collaboration with MTV, Laguna Beach is a virtual resort, created to appeal to a young crowd. Hence the nude beach, presumably. But cinema-lovers of all ages will want to keep their clothes on and head over to the beach's impressive cinema screen, where previous highlights have included screenings from the New York Museum of the Moving Images' machinima festival. An odd thing about Laguna Beach in Second Life is that it started life as a completely separate online world that MTV hoped would prove to be a rival to the work of Linden Lab. Only after MTV saw more and more of their audience choosing to live in-world rather than hanging out on MTV.com did the music-video giant decide that if you can't beat 'em ...

One-off screenings

As well as Second Life's permanent movie theatres, there are countless one-off screenings of films in-world. Some of these are illegal – and Linden Lab has had to work hard to prevent Residents streaming copyrighted movies onto screens on their land – but the majority are just the work of film fans and amateur directors sharing their passion with others.

One great example of what Second Life is capable of came when a group of film lovers took over the top floor of the Elbow Room bar to put on an interactive version of *Mystery Science Theatre* (*MST*). For anyone not up on their American cult-TV history, *MST* was a weekly cable programme in which a man and his robot sidekicks (don't ask) were imprisoned on a spaceship (really, don't ask) and forced to provide sarcastic voiceovers to cheesy American sci-fi films of the 1950s. In *MST*, Second Life-style, the fifties movies were still there – projected onto a white wall – but instead it was the Residents themselves who provided the voiceovers.

To find out when the next Second Life version of *MST* is happening, or when any of the other in-world film screenings are being shown, keep an eye on **http://secondlife.com/events**.

Culture

Low culture, high culture, and every point in between – it's all present and correct in Second Life. Museums for every taste (from modern art to sci-fi), cultural events, debates, exhibitions, scientific experiments – even zoos – mean you'll be learning something new every minute.

Galleries and cultural centres

Parioli

Modelled loosely on the neighbourhood in Rome, Parioli is one of the most popular, and beautifully constructed, centres of art in-world. The first thing you'll notice when you arrive is the fruit barrow, laden with nature's bounty, and with a young monochrome girl kneeling beside it, holding a shiny red apple. Why, if it isn't Audrey Hepburn! 'Please tip my cart,' begs the sign, 'or take home one of my daughters.' The fruit-seller is Audrey's father! In Parioli, even the tip jars are arty. With L\$25 spent on a cardboard cut-out of the star of

Breakfast at Tiffany's, it's time to take to the skies and fly to the undoubted highlight of Parioli – Bruno Echegaray's immersive spheres exhibition. Every so often something in Second Life makes you stop and think 'wow' as you realize that you're witnessing something that couldn't be accomplished in the real world. And the spheres will do exactly that.

About four times the height of your average avatar, these giant floating spheres contain amazing 360-degree works of art pasted on their inside. To view them, you simply hop inside the sphere, sit down, and spin around. And if you get bored of one view, simply click the wall for another one. Great stuff.

Fans of English football will be amused at what lies within the big glass-roofed building next to the spheres. It's an

Italian indoor football pitch, surrounded by posters promoting – who else – Chelsea. You'll need to provide your own ball.

Back in search of art, and across the main square (past the McDonald's – no, really) you'll find a gigantic gallery featuring the works of DanCoyote Antonelli. Antonelli's work is in a style described as Hyperformalism, which apparently is a 'mass art phenomenon consisting of scores of personal computer users generating abstract, often spacially unique artworks with software tools.' Whatever. It's very pretty.

And before you leave, don't forget to check out the working metro train underneath the sim's town hall.

The Seacliffe Gallery

The Seacliffe Gallery is a thing of real beauty. Appearing as if the entire building has been carved from a piece of a tree, and then connected with huge sheets of glass, the gallery is worth visiting even if you don't look at a single piece of art. But look you must, as the works here represent a huge spectrum of styles, from contemporary to classic, from abstract to still life.

If you're used to wandering around traditional gallery spaces, you'll find the Seacliffe either incredibly liberating or hugely frustrating. There are no real floors or ceilings, just a series of platforms joined together by twisty stairs that you have to work really hard not to fall down.

The only real criticism is that there isn't more information about the pieces on display and none appears to be on sale. A missed opportunity, but still a great way to kill some in-world time.

Phoenicia Centre for Contemporary Art

In stark contrast to the Seacliffe, the Phoenicia Centre models itself on a traditional gallery with three floors of soft arches, white walls, and high ceilings all serving to keep the attention firmly on the contemporary artworks on display. And what striking works they are – with photography particularly in evidence, along with some stunning Real Life paintings transported in-world. Phoenicia also hosts art openings and special events throughout the year – and all works are for sale if you've got some spare Linden dollars and a cultural bent.

Enigmatic Artworks

At the grand opening of this gallery of painting and photography, over L$15,000 worth of art was sold, giving you an idea of its popularity. Based on the waterlogged Infamy Sim (specifically designed to be covered in boring old water rather than complicated trees and things so that the graphics loaded quickly – handy when you've come to see artwork), the gallery is designed to optimize the browsing experience for art lovers. As a result there are no windows (again, quicker loading times and fewer distractions from the work), plain walls, and high ceilings. But if the surroundings are plain, the art is anything but – with dazzling digital photography and a monthly themed exhibition on the first floor. Like all good gallery owners, Enigmatic's owner, Amie Collingwood, personally reviews the portfolios of all of the artists who wish to exhibit in the space and only accepts those that fit in with Enigmatic's sensibilities. The result is a stunning space, filled with high-resolution artwork and a recipe for financial ruin if you don't keep a tight grip on the purse strings.

PartICLE Accelerator

Interesting one, this. Artist and gallery owner Fau Ferdinand designed her PartICLE Accelerator gallery based on the Real Life particle accelerator that she could see out of her bedroom window growing up in Israel. But where the Koffler accelerator at the Weizmann Institute of Science was a place of scientific experimentation, the PartICLE gallery has somewhat more artistic ambitions. The work on display spans a wide range of styles, reflecting Ferdinand's own refusal to settle on a single style for more than a few months. As she explained to *Slatenight* magazine (**http://www.slatenight.com**), 'I get bored with style pretty quickly and change it very often'. Consistency's loss is art's gain.

Free Culture

The Free Culture Event Group is not a place, but rather a group of people within Second Life who have made it their business to organize and attend free cultural events in-world. The group is closely affiliated with the Creative Commons movement – an increasingly influential group of academics and creative types who have invented a new form of copyright licence that allows work to be shared, without releasing it entirely into the public domain. Events organized by the group so far include book discussions by authors such as Ellen Ullman and Cory Doctorow, talks and debates by academics and artists, and the Creative Commons Art Exhibition. To find out more about Free Culture events in-world simply use the 'groups' tag within Second Life's search function and search for Free Culture.

Kula – Creative Commons Island

Creative Commons has embraced Second Life in a huge way (and vice versa). Kula Island is home to some of the most ground-breaking free art you'll find in-world, with all manner of constantly changing exhibitions, displays, and installations.

On arrival, after clicking the play button on your music controls to hear the free tunes pumping out of the island's giant speakers, your first stop should undoubtedly be the Creative Commons Art Gallery. Designed to encourage Second Life Residents not just to see art, but to share it, the gallery hosts events like Remix Art where artists are invited to take other people's art and to remix it into works of their own. These works are then displayed in-world, for free.

If photography's your thing, then across the other side of the main square you'll find a second art stage, this time dedicated to images 'snapped' from within Second Life itself. From action shots taken during in-world gigs to breathtaking scenic images, it's hard not to be impressed by the abilities of photographers who can compose, light, and take this kind of photograph in a virtual environment.

Then, if all this talk of Creative Commons has got you

curious, wander over to the island's open-air lecture theatre, complete with killer acoustics and giant projection screen.

But nothing – nothing – can possibly compare with the pièce de résistance of Kula: the full-sized avatar chess set. Oh yes! Simply grab a couple of dozen friends (or join the Avatar Chess group to make new ones) and download a full-body chess-piece costume for each player. Then, once you've chosen your costume (a rook, say, or a queen), get changed and stand in your place on the board. From then on in, it's just like a standard game of chess with the players moving themselves around the board according to the standard rules. Of course it takes a bit of coordination to work out a strategy for your entire team – but that's half the fun.

Fark Central

OK, putting this one in the culture section is pushing it, but it certainly gives an insight into culture *of sorts*. For the uninitiated, Drew Curtis' Fark.com is a place for American (mainly) teenagers and college students to post links to funny, crazy, or salacious links from around the web. Already one of the highest-trafficked sites of its type on the Internet, it was only a matter of time before it moved in-world. Definitely one aimed at teenage boys, Fark Central is decorated like an adolescent's bedroom with girly posters plastering the walls and even a strange hidden bed thing for when occupants get lucky. Which they probably won't.

Hipcast Conference and Expo Center

An upscale conference and expo centre available for companies to hire to stage in-world technology events. But even if you're not planning on attending an event the Hipcast Center is well worth a visit. On arrival, make sure you take a look behind you to see the luxury yacht moored on the jetty, then wander down the main approach admiring the futuristic architecture and sheer scale of the place. And then get yourself over to **http://hipcastexpo.wordpress.com** for a full run-down of the events available to attend. Warning: if you're not a technologically minded person you probably won't understand the titles of half the events, let alone the content.

Museums

Given that Second Life has only been around for about half a decade, it's not surprising that most in-world museums refer to things in the real world. But what a mixed bag of things! From the painstaking reproduction of St Paul's Cathedral to the even more painstakingly recreated *Star Trek* museum, you'll soon find yourself taking a trip back to both the past, and the future.

The International Spaceflight Museum

Located on Spaceport Alpha, the International Spaceflight Museum is home to a huge exhibition of rockets and rocketry and a fully functioning planetarium – and both are amazing

pieces of work.

The highlight of the museum proper is the chance to take a ride into low-earth orbit on an enormous rocket. A sign at the entrance warns riders not to board if they have a fear of vacuums, small spaces, or exploding – so you know this is the real deal, not just a simulator. After buckling up and going through some important pre-flight checks, it's time to experience 7gs, a trip 400 kilometres above the surface of the world, and some absolutely breathtaking views of the Grid. Once you reach low orbit, there's even more to see: there are models of the Hubble Space Telescope and the International Space Station for starters, and – this being Second Life – the adventure doesn't stop there. By clicking on the models of planets scattered around in low orbit, you can visit Mercury or Venus and see models of satellites and orbiters that have been there before you, in the real world.

And then, when you're done boldly going, if you don't fancy taking the Shuttle back you can always fly, or teleport or even cloud surf and parachute back down to earth.

Unbelievably, even after visiting the outer reaches of the solar system, you've still barely scratched the surface of the International Spaceflight Museum. Before you leave be sure to check out the simulation boxes which allow you to experience being inside a Space Shuttle, or the stunning circle of rockets, or of course the Planetarium, where space experts lecture on everything from the origins of the cosmos to whether the Moon landings were faked. (The answer is no, apparently. But then they *would* say that.)

The Star Trek Museum

If you prefer your space travel with less science fact and more science fiction, then get yourself along to the Star Trek Museum. Easy as it is to wonder if there's anything geekier than a Star Trek Museum in a virtual world (incidentally, the answer, again, is no), it's also hard not to marvel at the effort that has gone into producing the exhibition. For a start, every aspect of the series – and its crafts and worlds – are painstakingly detailed. Ever wondered what a photon torpedo looks like? (Pretend you have.) Then just click on the relevant panel on the wall for photos, stats, and much, much more. Then head over to the Star Trek planetarium to seek out brave new worlds, Kirk/Picard style.

Close Encounter UFO Museum

Still not bored of spaceships? OK, then finish your day by popping into the Close Encounter UFO Museum, containing everything you could ever possibly, possibly want to know about unidentified flying things in all their forms. The truth is in there.

Meteroa

From the outer reaches of space, head to the deepest depths of the ocean in Meteroa, the official sim of America's National Oceanic and Atmospheric Administration (crazy name, crazy guys). Highlights of the museum include a frighteningly realistic tsunami – and hurricane – simulator, a ride in a submarine, and all manner of demonstrations of what happens when the sea, and the weather, conspire to make things deeply unpleasant for humans.

St Paul's Cathedral

Designed in the real world by Sir Christopher Wren, who completed the work in 1710, St Paul's Cathedral is one of London's most famous landmarks. In Second Life too, St Paul's is a formidable building, with its imposing dome and towering marble pillars. Once inside, the first thing that strikes you is how much work has gone into reproducing the interior, right down to the altar with a copy of the Bible that can be clicked on to get a bite-sized paragraph of Christianity. And if you don't mind incurring the wrath of the curator, you can fly up inside the dome and study the stunning carvings at

close hand – or even head back outside and take a walk across the roof. But before you leave make sure you drop some Linden dollars into the tip jar to support the upkeep of the building. Your reward will be in Second Life heaven.

September 11th Memorial

The impact of 9/11 doesn't stop just because you're in a virtual world, as this moving memorial to the events of September 11th shows. Two tall, ghostly towers stretch up into the sky while around the base a visitors' centre provides information about the terror attacks including a list of everyone who died in the two towers. Adjoining buildings contain more information and photographs ensuring that even in-world, we'll never forget.

Books and Literature

Books may be the total opposite of Second Life – analogue, linear, even stuffy – but the literature they contain is more than well represented in-world. Which is possibly not surprising, given that the whole concept for Second Life was inspired by a book. From contemporary authors like Neal Stephenson and Warren Ellis to old masters like Tolkien (through the J. R. R. Tolkien Education Centre), Second Life provides a veritable in-world treasure trove.

Snow Crash sampler

There can be no better place to start a literary tour of Second Life than Neal Stephenson's *Snow Crash*, the book that started it all. Penguin, Stephenson's publisher, apparently agree as it has created a virtual sampler of the book in-world. Fans can download sample chapters from the book, watch video clips, and follow a special link to the Penguin website where a hard copy of the title is available at a discount. Penguin promises that *Snow Crash* is just the first of several books that it's hoping to move in-world, and other publishers are looking to follow suit – so watch this space.

Snowbooks

From *Snow Crash* to Snowbooks. One of the nice things about Second Life is that it creates an almost level playing field, with publishers large and small sitting alongside each other displaying their literary wares. And so it is that award-winning independent UK publisher Snowbooks has set up camp in the snowy peaks of Sled. All of the company's titles – from fiction-bestseller *Adept* to the unauthorized Peter Cook biography *How Very Interesting!* . . . – are available to browse (sort of – just the back-cover blurb for now) and Residents can even grab their own Snowbooks bookshelf, loaded with titles, ready to bolt on a handy wall. Emma Barnes, Snowbooks' MD, promises that more innovations are on the cards but even now it's a great place to find some new authors you might not otherwise have heard of.

Info Island

Home to the Second Life Library project, Info island is in fact a collection of small themed libraries, each dealing with a different type of fiction or non-fiction information. It's still in the early stages of construction but if you're curious about developments then the creators have an excellent website at **http://www.infoisland.org** where you can keep up to date with what's going on.

Libraries already in existence within Info Island include . . .

The Medical Library

Developed by a medical librarian from the Netherlands, the Medical Library provides links to useful medical sources on the Internet, presumably for use if your avatar should become ill.

The History Gallery Garden

The History Gallery Garden features two different women (changing frequently) from the nineteenth century with profiles of their life, photos, and other historical data to give an in-depth introduction to what life was like in that period. The garden is nicely designed too and so is well worth a wander around, whether you're a history buff or not.

Murder at Mystery Manor

One for murder-mystery fans, Mystery Manor is a castle packed to the rafters with information on mystery and horror authors. Diligent investigators may also discover the secret tunnel underneath the castle leading to . . . we couldn't possibly ruin the ending.

At the time of writing the library was expanding in the hope of 'extending the programs currently offered online to librarians and library users of the Second Life virtual reality game.' Game, indeed!

New World Notes Book Prototype Expo

King of the literary nerds, it's no surprise that Cory Doctorow (one of the pioneers of publishing under Creative Commons licences – see 'Galleries and Cultural Centres', p. 160) has come to town in Second Life with his novel *Someone Comes To Town, Someone Leaves Town*. In 2006, the Book Prototype Expo played host to Doctorow, putting on various events to promote the novel including a virtual book-signing and even a competition for Residents to recreate the book's cover in-world. One of the most innovative recreations was produced by dressing up an avatar as the main character from the cover and having her pose in various positions while another avatar photographed her. Today the Expo has long finished, but the land remains so is worth keeping an eye on for future literary extravaganzas – and for the Doctorow fans who regularly show up in search of their hero's avatar.

The _black*library*

Part library, part arts centre, The _black*library* is an interesting experiment to examine how information stored on the web in text form can be represented in a traditional library format in-world. Or, to put it another way, it looks like a library and it acts like a library with fiction and non-fiction 'books' (really text articles) available to read by clicking. But each book is, in reality, a link through to a website on the traditional Internet, where the text can be accessed. It's well worth checking out as an example of how Second Life, the real world, and the Internet can work together to make information easily accessible. The _black*library* also has a large lecture theatre that plays host to arts events which, again, examine the possibilities offered for arts and literature in-world. Oh, and there's a bar in the basement in which, in the words of the library's librarian, 'experiments in stupid jokes will be conducted'.

Shakespeare and Company Bookshop

Named after the famous bookshop in (real-world) Paris, the Shakespeare and Company Bookshop in the Mill Pond sim is home to a growing community of poetry lovers, thanks to the shop's weekly readings (which generally take the form of an avatar miming away to the author's Real Life voice). The shop, which looks more like a house where every wall is lined with books, was built by Grace McDunnough (aka Rhonda Lowry in the real world), who works for Turner Broadcasting

in New York. Lowry claims never to have visited the real thing in Paris, but rather fell in love with the idea of it and wanted to pay homage in-world.

The J. R. R. Tolkien Education Center

Given that the Tolkien Center hopes to encourage readers to discover the author's books, it's either a brilliant or a strange decision that all the images scattered around the sim are taken straight from the Hollywood film adaptations, rather than illustrations. Perhaps this is to snare younger readers who may have already seen the films, or perhaps it's because film stills look cool – either way, it's Peter Jackson all the way, photographically speaking. But the real draw of the Tolkien

Center is the wealth of information available about Middle-earth – the inhabitants, the history, and the adventures.

Also in the sim is a recreation of the Prancing Pony pub, complete with roaring fire, plates of food, and flagons of ale. There are even rooms upstairs if you fancy a lie down after all the excitement.

Experiments and Curios

If you thought the real world was odd, wait till you get a load of what Second Life has to offer. Like an enormous laboratory, packed with mad scientists with crazy hair, there's a curious experiment around every corner in-world. Not all of which are *entirely* academic.

The Crooked House

Robert A. Heinlein, in his somewhat off-the-wall sci fi story "—And He Built a Crooked House—" (dashes and quotes author's own), tells of an architect who builds a four-dimensional house which, after an earthquake, folds in on itself into a continuous loop. Of course, in reality such a house wouldn't be possible, earthquake or not, thanks to a little thing called physics. But if we know anything about Second Life it's that little things like physics – and even reality – have no place in-world. And so it is that Seifert Surface, a graduate maths student at Stanford, has created the world's first working example of Heinlein's vision – an endless, continuous house that requires you to leave your sense of logic, as well as your shoes, at the door. On entering the house, things look normal enough – a big marble table sits in the foyer, and on the table is a button. But pushing the button – that's when things go mental. Doors lead to rooms that you've already been in, windows have views that change depending where you've come from previously, and ladders and hatches that should lead to one place actually lead to quite another. You're both stuck and able to walk forever all at the same time. Take a packed lunch, you'll be there some time.

The ANWR Oil Rig

In what is perhaps a cheeky dig at President Bush's oil-drilling ambitions in the Arctic, the ANWR in the ANWR Oil Rig stands for the Arctic National Wildlife Reserve. But instead of drilling for oil, the ANWR rig drills for prims – the building blocks that make up the structures in Second Life. Watch in awe as the huge pumps bring block after block from the sea bed and then – well – watch some more. It's not exactly the most useful experiment on Second Life, but it's certainly one of the more ambitiously pointless.

Not long ago the rig was in danger of being deleted as part of a restructuring of the Grid by Linden Lab. But thanks to intensive Resident lobbying, the rig, and the pipeline that connects it to the neighbouring sim, has been saved for posterity. Hurrah! Let's hope the same happens to the Arctic National Wildlife Reserve.

Democracy Island

OK, calling democracy an experiment may be stretching it, but what the New York Law School-based makers of Democracy Island are trying to do is certainly ambitious. Calling itself a 'do tank' (as opposed to a think tank), the island aims to give a platform to interest groups and campaigners who can then consult with – and campaign to – the public to shape policy and opinion on a wide range of subjects. Events already held on the island include the rulemaking fair – a country-fair-themed event where Residents can stroll from stand to stand, considering a range of different proposals for laws or rules, before voting on which they believe would benefit society. But there's more. Democracy Island is in fact made up of a collection of smaller islands around a central hub. Each of these sub-islands has a different theme and aim including:

Landing Lights Island
Where Residents can help design and build a recreation park to be built in Queens, New York. Designs can be planned, built, and saved – and then shared with other budding designers.

Governance in SL Island
Where Residents can debate the question of law and government in-world.

Nanotech Island

The part of Democracy Island where tiny technology is the order of the day. Watch out for grey goo (p. 34).

Audio-Visual Island

Does exactly what it says on the tin. A place for audio and video presentations of all types including presentations by special-interest groups and audio/video lectures for and by students at New York Law School.

Projects Island

Land made available to rent for smaller experiments and presentations.

DOT Island

Short for 'Department of Transportation'; DOT Island is where American public and private transportation policy is test driven.

Imagination Breeding and Zoo

Awww. Imagine a petting zoo where instead of goats and hens and rabbits and the like, you could pet lions and tigers and bears (oh my!). Well, imagine no longer. At this colourful zoo – designed to bring out the child in you – you can get up close and personal with almost any wild creature you can imagine; take them for a ride, race them on the race track. Or even

plonk down some Linden dollars and buy yourself an entire menagerie of creatures to start your own safari park.

And did we mention the tricks? Oh yes, these aren't just ordinary animals – there's an elephant that juggles, a talking penguin, even armed ducks that threaten to blow you to pieces with rocket launchers. You'll probably want to feed them some bread before they get angry.

The Independent State of Caledon

The nineteenth-century independent nation state of Caledon is part theme park, part museum, and part collection of science experiments. Actually Caledon is a collection of Victorian-themed sims where steam powers almost everything, huge metal (!) airships float around the sky, and the ruling steward lives at 10 Downing Street.

Caledon is one of those fast-growing sims that are best explored to find the latest creations and advancements, but highlights include:

The tram system
Currently operating three routes in Port Caledon, Caledon Smuggler's Cay, and Caledon Victoria City.

The train system
Connecting five sims, the Caledon train system is a truly impressive piece of engineering. And of course, this being Caledon the whole thing is powered by steam. Choo choo!

Hot-air balloons
Built to be shared, these multi-seater balloons are a great way to explore Caledon by air. Simply nominate a pilot, master some simple voice commands, and it's up, up, and away.

The Library
The whole point of Caledon is that it's a true representation (apart, perhaps, from the metal airships), so it's important that Residents know how to act like people who lived in the nineteenth century. So step forward the Caledon library, containing all of the information and advice you could possibly need to know about how to fit in, in and around Caledon.

The Babbage Difference Engine

This Real-Life precursor of the modern computer was invented by Charles Babbage. Without it there would be no calculators, no computers, and – gasp – no Second Life. And so it only seems appropriate that Caledon is home to the in-world version of this iconic machine. We're not sure if it's powered by steam.

The Grail

It's always nice to stumble across something that has absolutely no function other than to look pretty. And the Grail is one of those places. Designed to be a beautiful, futuristic castle in the sky, with no corners and a stunningly beautiful elevator, it meets all these goals perfectly. Nothing more, nothing less.

Chapter Eight:
Going Native

'Are you serious? This is working like SH*T. I'm so tired of having smoke blown up my A*S. The wonderful new update is going to be soooooo great. Yea right. It sucks more now than ever. Do the Lindens know anything about testing before they apply the changes? I cant believe how much this sucks now. Its unbelievable to me. Nothing works. I'm invisible, my money is gone, nothing in my inventory is there. What are we to do? The amount of complaints is amazing and still nothing gets done.'
— *Cathy Ryder, The Second Life Forum*

Second Life can be incredibly frustrating. At the moment and for the immediate future, the technology simply isn't able to cope with the collective imagination of millions of Residents. As well as often unmanageable amounts of lag, which can make the most basic tasks feel like they're being performed in an invisible lake of molasses, there are frequent technical issues, Linden-side. During the time we spent writing this book, there were two seemingly quite major updates to the software and some very serious problems with search functionality. Naturally Residents get very frustrated with this. It

would be like waking up one day in Real Life and finding out when you got to the station that the trains weren't running. None of them, for the foreseeable future. And someone had glued your legs to the floor.

Residents' frustrations are reflected in the titles of threads in the Second Life forum. Here are just a selection of conversations from the last couple of days in the Technical Issues forum: 'SL Support is not responding to my ISSUES!', 'av bug?', 'critical error login failures', 'crashing A LOT since the update', 'prims gathering around my waist', 'small objects vanishing', 'everybody is bald!'

We have no doubt that in time the vast majority of these problems will be solved. Graphics cards and processors are getting more powerful every day and the hardware industries are working as hard as they possibly can to keep up with MMORPG developers and keep users happy. But for the moment, in Second Life, very basic problems will persist, and with shocking regularity.

The point is, if you can cope with all of this, if you can see beyond the sometimes sensational frustrations of everyday existence within Second Life, then you probably have what it takes – whatever that is – to count yourself a Resident. It's probably time to go native.

This chapter, then, deals with the basic things you may want to consider once you realize that Second Life may actually have more to offer than First Life.

Money Matters

One of the most important things to do – and often the hardest – when you're moving to a new country is set up a bank account. But fortunately, in Second Life it's a doddle.

To own land in-world you need to upgrade to a premium Second Life account for (currently) US$9.95 a month. Doing so makes you the equivalent of a naturalized Second Life citizen with all the benefits that brings. Benefits like a L$1000 sign-up bonus plus a weekly stipend from Linden of L$300, land ownership (or, more accurately, leasing) rights, and the ability to build on that land.

But most importantly, it gives you the feeling of superiority over mere basic Residents that money can't buy. Suddenly you feel like you're a proper Second Lifer. Now all you need to do is find somewhere nice to live.

House Hunting

There are two main ways to get property in Second Life. The first is to rent an existing property (or space within a property) from another Resident; the second is to rent some land of your own and build a place yourself.

Renting Existing Property

Renting existing property is a quick and easy way to get into the Second Life property market. It requires no building skills, it's flexible (rent terms can be as short as a few days), and yet it still gives you a place to call home.

The ease with which properties can be rented in Second Life has created a growing holiday-let industry, where Residents can rent space on tropical islands and other picturesque sims for short-term stays. Of course, given the ease with which you can teleport around the world, it's reasonable to question the logic of needing a holiday home. But of all the shared traits of Second Life Residents, logic is not one of them.

Finding places in-world that are available to rent is a simple matter of clicking the 'search' button in the Second Life software, choosing the 'classifieds' tab, and then selecting 'property rentals' from the drop-down menu. You'll be presented with a list of places available for rent, and the price. But remember, at all times: caveat rentor.

Popular rental spots in Second Life …

Legacy Gardens II (on South Pacific II)

Legacy Gardens is literally a cottage industry, letting delightful fairy-themed cottages to Residents who like to dress up in wings and sparkly shoes. Admittedly, the trees, lavish gardens, and lots and lots of marble all add up to making Legacy Gardens II appear something like a cross between a garden centre and a retirement village – but at least (as in a retirement village) you can be sure of your safety thanks to the development's twenty-four-hour security-guard coverage, with help summoned by just a mouse-click.

Lance Lasalle (on Caribbean Paradise)

Those with expensive tastes and a yearning for yachting will want to seriously consider a 'VIP' apartment or beach house on Lance Lasalle. Eschewing pushy real-estate agents (so common!), the island features the far-from-tacky 'rent-a-matic', which with a simple click provides everything you need to become the proud occupant of a beachside place to call home. The boats moored in the harbour give a clear idea of the calibre of Resident the owners are hoping to attract. And the fact that none of the yachts appears to be occupied gives a hint at how successful they've been in attracting them.

Still – lovely scenery, particularly if you want to escape the crowds.

Surf Island

A dedicated island, promising 'boating . . . a gazebo . . . dolphins . . . monkeys . . .', everything you could possibly want from a new neighbourhood, then. With only eight homes on the entire island and rents starting at L$2500 per week, Surf is definitely one for the well-heeled – but if you've got the means then it's certainly an impressive address. Palm trees sway on every corner, mountains loom in the distance, and everywhere you step there's the crunch of sand beneath your feet. The homes themselves have all mod cons and there's even a huge communal campfire – perfect for bonding with your new neighbours.

The Lofts at Mill Pond

At the lower end of the price scale, the Lofts at Mill Pond are ideal starter apartments for new Residents. With great views of Mill Pond itself and free prim building blocks to develop your property, rents start at just L$500 a week.

This Land is My Land

Renting is fun – but at the end of the day, you're renting someone else's dream. Someone else's house design, on someone else's landscaped desert island. To truly go native it's vital to own (or more accurately, rent) your own piece of the Grid and to construct your own place from scratch. The nice thing about land in Second Life is that there are very few local laws or planning restrictions. Providing you have the space you can build a shack, a palace, a shop, a mall – even a theme park. It's a terrible cliché, but in this case it's true: the possibilities are limited only by your imagination.

First Land

As we mentioned earlier, Chinese businesswoman and Second Life real-estate queen Anshe Chung announced in December 2006 that the value of her land and other assets in-world had reached $1,000,000. That's one million real US dollars. There's no doubt about it, the relative scarcity of land in-world is pushing prices up. Aware that soaring land prices are making it hard for new Residents to get a foot on the property ladder, Linden has introduced a First Land scheme. The scheme offers first-time buyers 512 square metres of land for L$1 per square metre and is only available to those who have never owned any kind of in-world land before.

To find First Land, use the land option in the search panel and choose 'first land' from the drop-down menu. First Land is subject to availability so you might have to be patient to get the land you want – but at L$512, you can't argue with the price.

Buying or Renting Land from Residents

If your ambitions reach beyond the limitations of First Land and you want to get hold of land that meets your exact speci-fications, then you'll need to buy it from a Resident. Fortunately the land market in Second Life is incredibly fluid so there's plenty to choose from, even if prices are starting to look a bit off-putting.

One way to keep costs down is to rent land from another landowner. This has the benefit of a lower cost of entry but also means that the land isn't really yours and as such you'll be at the mercy of your landlord when it comes to things like rent increases. Land available to rent can be found in the classifieds search panel, by selecting 'land rental'.

If you've got your heart set on buying then you have two

options – buying directly and buying by auction. To buy directly, go to the search area in the Second Life software, select the 'land sales' tab and choose either your price range or the size of land you're looking for (or both). A list of available land will be shown, along with information on where it's situated and the option to teleport in and have a look around. Payment for purchased land is made directly to the vendor using Linden dollars. Buying land at auction gives added flexibility in terms of both price and also method of paying. A drop-down menu in the 'land sales' tab gives you the option to show ongoing and upcoming land auctions and you'll find sales in both Linden and US dollars.

Land fees

No matter how you buy your land, if you want to keep using it, you'll need to pay Linden an ongoing Land Use Fee (also called a Tier Fee). Land Use Fees are the nearest the Grid has to a property tax. Land fees are billed in US$ based on the peak (or maximum) amount of land you hold in any thirty-day billing period. The first 512 square metres (handily the basic amount you can buy under the First Land scheme) is not eligible for Land Use Fees and the fees are tiered so the amount you pay scales down as you acquire more land. The current Land Use Fees rate can be found at **http://secondlife. com/whatis/landpricing.php**. At the time of writing, fees started at $5 pcm for 512 square metres (over and above your free 512 square metres) and go up to $195 pcm for 65,536 square metres (equal to owning an entire region).

The History of Second Life, Part Five: The CopyBot Wars

November 2006 saw the attack of the CopyBot in Second Life. In layman's terms, what this meant was that any Resident with the skill and desire to do so was suddenly able to replicate any three-dimensional object in the metaverse. This meant that the whole economy was in jeopardy. Imagine how Adidas would feel, for example, if one day its enormously sought-after a3 Microride sneakers were suddenly hanging from every tree in the metaverse, free for anyone who fancied a pair. More importantly, small independent retailers were suddenly in a position where their very second livelihood could be taken away from them.

The software which allowed this to happen was created by libsecondlife, an organization working with the full consent of Linden Lab with the aim of integrating Second Life with the rest of the Internet. When it was originally built, the CopyBot had code written into it which would always ask permission before copying something. Unfortunately, the open nature of libsecondlife's work means that everything they do is open-sourced, so the CopyBot was copied and the permissions code removed.

After a considerable degree of mayhem during which hundreds of businesses stopped trading, the metaverse became over-stuffed with replica objects, servers crashed, and Linden Lab called in the FBI, the Lindens eventually came up with a short-term solution. It made unauthorized use of the CopyBot a bannable violation of Second Life's terms of service.

Building

So, you're the proud owner of some land. Now, if you've still got some Linden dollars spare (and let's hope you have), it's time to get building your dream castle in the sky. Or on the beach. Or under the sea. Although there are some stunningly complex structures in-world, they're all made out of the same raw material: primitives, or 'prims'. Prims are the building blocks of Second Life and are basic shapes that can be connected together, stretched, and otherwise modified to create structures. Everything you see in-world, from the beach ball or party hat that comes as standard with your avatar (see the inventory option in the Second Life software) to the Spaceflight Museum (p. 164), is built out of prims.

For an amusing – if not entirely scientifically accurate – representation of where prims come from, see the ANWR Oil Rig in the 'Entertainment' chapter (p. 175).

Learning to build

It's only right that the best way to learn how to build in Second Life is by watching, reading, and taking part in the large number of regular tutorials that are hosted in-world. A good place to start is . . .

The Ivory Tower Library of Primitives

A magnificent building (as is only fitting), the Ivory Tower Library of Primitives is designed to represent an in-game Tower of Babel. The tower houses a massive centre of information about the Second Life in-world building system including a totally interactive tutorial on every aspect of prim manipulation.

Tutorials and one-to-one assistance

The official Second Life events list (**http://secondlife.com/events**) offers a daily listing of in-world building tutorials. Simply choose 'educational' from the drop-down menu to see what's available. There's generally at least one event a day for budding builders.

Sandboxes: full of sand and furries, signifying nothing

Having mastered the basics, before you start building your five-storey bachelor pad with swimming pool on the roof and mermaids cavorting with ducks on the patio, you'll probably want to have a bit of a practice. Fortunately Second Life has set aside huge sections of desert for this very purpose.

The sandboxes are pieces of barren land where Residents can – at no cost – practise building houses, shops, cars, mermaids . . . whatever they fancy. And then, twice a day – regular as clockwork – the whole thing is emptied of contents and the building begins again.

Even if you're not planning to do any building, sandboxes are great places to wander around, admiring the handiwork of others. You never know whether you'll stumble across a skyscraper in the making, or an enormous talking robot called Alice who answers your questions like a precocious four-year-old with learning difficulties.

Finding a sandbox is as simple as popping up the search panel, choosing the 'places' tab and searching 'sandboxes'. But a few popular ones to get you started include . . .

Goguen

One of the biggest sandboxes, Goguen has the curious honour of having once had its own army to protect it. Or more accurately, its own detachment of the Second Life Alliance to keep out any troublemakers. But, as discussed in the 'People' chapter (p. 66), they've gone now.

The Weapons Testing Sandbox

Designed specially for testing weapons, this is the place to go if you've made, or bought, yourself something capable of inflicting harm. Be warned, testing weapons in a non-weapons sandbox is a pretty effective way of getting yourself deported from Second Life.

Sandbox rules . . .

* No buying or selling. Sandboxes are trade-free zones.
* No advertising.
* No gambling.
* No weapons (outside dedicated weapons-testing sandboxes)

Sandbox etiquette . . .

* Respect the efforts of others. Don't get in the way or disturb people when they're building. Don't give them any grief, in other words.

* Tidy up after yourself. Although most sandboxes automatically clear at set times, leaving things behind causes clutter and increases lag for others. However much fun you have rezzing the *Titanic*, make sure you put it away again when you're done.

* Don't build at the point where you arrive. Lots of other people will arrive at the same point and your building will get in their way.

* No ducking, no diving, no bombing, no heavy petting.

Earning Your Keep

The Second Life economy is largely built on the blood and sweat of entrepreneurs – individual Residents starting their own businesses and earning Linden dollars to support their in-world lives. But a growing number of Residents who have no interest in starting full-blown businesses are taking part-time work to make ends meet.

One of the most popular types of work, perhaps unsurprisingly, is in the adult industry. There's something much easier about taking your electronic clothes off in-world than there is in the real world. Likewise there's far less stigma about acting as a stripper or hostess (or host, of course) in a Second

Life nightclub. And yet the money on offer to Residents who are willing to shake their stuff for paying punters is not to be sleazed – sorry – sneezed at. See the 'After Dark' chapter (p. 206) for an idea of what's on offer.

But if you're too prudish for sex work, there are still loads of opportunities for part-time employment, especially if you have real-world skills that you're willing to use. To find details of available jobs, use the classifieds tab in the search panel and choose 'employment' from the drop-down menu.

Unskilled labour

With more and more companies opening shops in-world (see the 'Shopping and Commerce' chapter, p. 110), there's always work for shop assistants who are able to demonstrate good product knowledge and provide service with a smile. Likewise even Second Life nightclubs, bars, and private property require bouncers and security guards.

Skilled labour

Skills are where the real money is in-world. If you're a skilled designer or prim builder or a gifted animator, then companies of all sizes are queuing up for help in building their in-world outlets. Likewise if you're a talented DJ, the burgeoning in-world club scene offers plenty of opportunity to earn, either through paid gigs or via tips from appreciative fans.

Settling Down

OK, so you've found a job, you've found yourself somewhere to live, now all you really need is that special someone to whom you can devote your second self. Someone to spend your Second Life with.

Here we'll be talking primarily about emotions, psychology, and practicalities by the way, rather than about sex. If it's the raw titillation of pixel-on-pixel love action you're after, we suggest you hightail it to the 'After Dark' chapter (p. 206).

As has been mentioned before, the great thing about Second Life, the *only* thing about Second Life, really, is the people. It's the personalities you meet – the ones that invite you to their home for a chat and a cup of tea or into their hot-air balloons for a tour of the world and an impromptu sex change. If you spend a lot of time in Second Life, before very long you may very well meet someone you find yourself attracted to.

Now, this is where it starts to get strange. Psychologically.

Obviously, you're not really physically attracted to anyone – neither to the pixels with which the person you're actually talking to has chosen to represent themselves in-world, nor to the person him- or herself, because you've never met them, and any photos that have been shared can obviously be taken with a pinch of salt. Initially, at least.

So the attraction is based – as in all virtual or non-physical communication – on language. You're attracted to how this person – through their avatar – is relating to you. The things they're choosing to talk about and the way in which they're communicating them. The only way in which this is different from a chatroom or a forum, or even a paper correspondence in the old days of pen pals, is that in Second Life you have these little people running around acting out your fantasies.

It may seem ridiculous till you've actually tried it and become somewhat immersed, but you can actually tell a great deal about someone from the stuff their avatar gets up to. If they're the kind of person who sets about building a house and making it nice, for example, you can probably surmise a certain amount about their Real Life personality. Similarly if they're the kind of person who smashes through your front-room window on their Harley Davidson or insists on trying to get a ball-gag into your mouth while you're talking to them, there are clues in their behaviour.

Not that they'd do that in Real Life, of course, but at least you know that they'd kind of like to, that somewhere deep inside is that kind of urge, or at the very least they have that kind of imagination.

So it's easy to become attracted to a person. Plus, let's face it, it's easier than in Real Life too, because what you see of the person you're falling for is pixellated loveliness, not bedraggled or time-battered flesh and blood. And although you know this is a million miles from reality, there is a certain amount of suspension of disbelief here. You are, after all, playing a game. (No, come on. It's true. Let's own up at this stage, shall we? Second Life is a game. There. We've said it.)

Also, it's not really you who's getting to know this person. It's your avatar. There are distances operating and most people who become involved in Second Life do so in the full knowledge that this will never have any impact on their Real Lives.

One case in point is Bam Camus, joint owner of Intimate Moments, the romantic gardens site we looked at in the 'Key Places to Visit' chapter (p. 96). She has a long-standing relationship with her online partner, Ron Bijoux. They own Intimate Moments together. In March 2006, they became official partners. If you go to Bam's profile, you can read: 'I love you, my sweet Ron. You make Second Life. Your encouragement and support lift me up. This is our world.' However, in Real Life Bam has a high-profile job in the States as a headhunter, and a Real Life partner. She spends an average of around three hours a day in Second Life. Her Real Life partner knows all about Ron and apparently isn't remotely jealous. This is because, perhaps obviously, there is a distinction between Second Life and Real Life and they rarely overlap.

'There aren't many Real Life relationships here in Second Life,' she says. 'Most are just online. But I do have a friend who is going to marry her Second Life partner and I know another who has moved in with one.' Bam's friends are not alone. Phil Murdock and Snow Hare started out as neighbours in Second Life. Then they became online lovers. Then they started designing sex animations. Then they met and their love made the leap to reality. 'It was almost like meeting an old friend and a lot of the nervousness of a first date wasn't there,' Phil told Wagner Au in *New World Notes*. 'This medium definitely lets two people share their feelings and desires for one another and that is a powerful thing in itself.' Bam agrees. 'I may be an avatar and Ron may be an avatar but people are behind each and they have feelings.'

So the emotions which Second Life gives rise to are definitely real and can be extremely significant. Plus there is also the physical side. As we'll see when we come to talk about sex, the physical side is also real, or at least can be. We asked Bam about people pleasuring themselves as their avatars get down to it. 'Some do,' she said, 'some just pretend to.'

Marriage

When a couple in Second Life are properly committed to one another, they tend – if they are the marrying kind – to get married, or, to use in-world parlance, partnered. There are lots of chapels in Second Life but one of the more popular venues is Dane Zander's Lost Gardens of Apollo (p. 83). Fees from weddings are actually one of the main sources of funding for Zander's Gardens.

When official marriage was introduced into Second Life, it became another opportunity to make a fast Linden buck. This from the Second Life website: 'Partnering, like Real Life marriage, costs money. To create a partnership will cost each partner L$10. If you decide to divorce later, the person requesting the divorce will be charged L$25.'

Sometimes it almost seems like everybody is being exploited.

Fidelity

Every Second Life couple we spoke to insisted that they would be hurt if their virtual partner were unfaithful to them. And vice versa. Bam explained: 'If Ron was kissing someone without my knowledge I would be pissed. Cheating is defined as having relationships with others without your partner's knowledge. Ron and I have been together a long time. In Second Life time, forever.'

Under the circumstances, perhaps it's not surprising that there also exist private detectives. Markie Macdonald, for example. Markie set up shop as a private dick in December 2004. A few months later she told *The Times*, 'We have people in love and getting married in Second Life and getting married is a commitment not to be unfaithful. I could see people who were married in Second Life paying for dances, sex, etc., and thought "I wonder if their partner knows"'. And so it began.

What usually happens is that someone who suspects their partner of cheating will approach Macdonald, then she, or one of her many staff, will set a honey trap. This is where the suspected partner is approached by a sexy avatar. That avatar will make him- or herself available and . . . that's pretty much it. When they're going at it, that's the moment for the honey-trapper to teleport the suspicious partner direct to the scene of the crime of misplaced passion. Animatus interruptus. A panicky fumbling for the 'stop all animations' tab and it's time to start explaining.

Sometimes Second Life just seems too ridiculous for words, it has to be said. Try explaining to someone who knows nothing about it that all over the world there are pretend people working for a pretend detective agency, and that these pretend people then pretend to be someone else so that they can seduce other pretend people; and that those pretend people's partners will then pay them money and most probably get very upset.

Sometimes it really is difficult to get your head round.

Suffice to say, in Second Life, just as in First Life, your feelings can get you in an awful lot of trouble.

There is a lot to be said, however, for online relationships that never manage to permeate the real world and it'll be interesting to see what happens in the future with Second Life. Will couples like Bam and Ron prove more durable than their Real Life counterparts? It's an odd thought, but imagine you've gone through three marriages and you're nearing the end of your life on this planet. Let's say you're alone now, your kids have grown up and moved away – they don't phone, they don't write, they don't even email. To all intents and purposes, you're alone. But there is still someone, the one constant in your life since you met them in the mid-noughties on the Internet. Your virtual love. Your Second Life partner. They've been with you through thick and thin, in sickness and in health, through marriage, divorce, and ignominy. And they've stood by you. The cynics amongst you are thinking, 'Well, of course they've stood by you – because they haven't had to put up with your crap in the real world. They don't actually know who you really are.'

Well, yeah.

Good point.

Or is it?

Chapter Nine:
After Dark

As we've seen, most of Second Life is designated an adults-only universe. Which is kind of pointless considering (a) the rest of the Internet is jam-packed full of the most hideous gruesome Real Life awfulness, most of which is easily accessible by anyone who's even mildly curious, and (b) all anyone under eighteen has to do to take part in adult Second Life is lie about their age on sign-up. And after just an hour or two of walking round and eavesdropping, you know – you pray – that many of the Residents are actually naughty children doing exactly that.

However, from a responsible-adults-running-a-successful-business point of view, it does make sense to appear to be looking out for the innocent cherubs that haven't been corrupted by turning eighteen yet.

If you yourself are under eighteen, you should probably stop reading this book now too. Sorry. It's not for you.

In this chapter we'll be looking at the dark side of Second Life – the sex, the violence, the crime, the murder – and we may well be asking: Is it really necessary to abide by real-world laws in Second Life? Would it be too much to ask to have at least one sim devoted to drug-taking and necrophilia?

Then again, we may not.

First Base

When Second Life began, there was no sex. But as we've seen, one of the most interesting things about a world in which Residents create everything is that as long as they don't transgress any of the Big Six rules and regulations and have the skills necessary to build what they want, they can make it happen.

According to Wagner Au, 'Even during its test ("Beta") period in early 2003, people were having sex in Second Life, with attachable sex organs no less. I found this out very shortly after becoming Linden Lab's "embedded journalist" in Second Life, and one of the most well-known Beta Residents showed me a palace that was actually an orgy grotto. On the walls of the palace were screenshots of male and female avatars in various combinations, testimony to their erotic play – and quite a bit of patience. This was before custom animations, or poseballs, or any of the devices Residents use now to simulate sex. Instead, what they did then was manoeuvre their avatars like life-sized dolls into these positions, a decidedly less animated way of making love – but then, you just put more eroticism into the chat. I'm tempted to say people started having sex in Second Life the moment people were in Second Life, but I'll just note I saw it going on in the first few months of its infancy.'

In the summer of 2004, two Residents, Francis Chung and Laura Fauna, created what was probably the world's first reasonably realistic, non-stilted 3D synthetic hug. When two avatars wanted to hug, they would attach a transparent cube with an embedded animation script to themselves, then they would click on the animation, type in a few short text commands, and they were off, their virtual arms wrapped tight around their virtual bodies in a loving embrace. Chung and Fauna began selling the animations and suddenly Second Life was awash with virtual affection. Teledildonics was only a couple of years away.

But first it was up to two more Residents, Phil Murdock and his partner Snow Hare, to create an animation for Second Life's first kiss, which they did around a year later. The response from Residents was so great that they now own one of the most successful sex-animations stores in the whole of Second Life, the Empire Vendors Group.

Full Sex

So, let's get down to the nitty-gritty. Lots of people come to Second Life in the hope of getting laid. Don't worry. No one's going to judge you. No one's going to suspect that just because you want to have sex through a bunch of pixels, you can't find it in Real Life. But let's face it – that's very definitely the case with lots of the others. Not you, we know. The others.

As we've seen, all you need to do to have sex in Second Life is to find yourself a willing partner and a couple of poseballs. However, as we've also seen, genitals do help make the experience that extra bit more realistic. A good set of genitals will become increasingly excited the more you click on them. After a certain amount of clickage and a specified amount of time, the genitalia will emit a particle stream and orgasm sounds will be heard. And that's pretty much it.

Of course, Second Life sex does have a lot of advantages over Real Life sex. There are no sexually transmitted diseases. There is no impotence or frigidity. Also, there's none of that awkward fumbling that might potentially hamper relations in Real Life. There is not too much room for error in the animations, but if the concomitant conversation is not really going according to plan, you can always just turn off Second Life and pretend your computer crashed.

Teledildonics

Teledildonics in Second Life was pioneered by a robotics engineer called qDot. Taking his lead from the vibrating joysticks introduced to PlayStation 2 games, qDot developed what are essentially sex toys that can be controlled over the Internet. Using the vibration technology that was already in place, qDot wrote software which allowed what he describes as 'a full virtual sex system' to be installed in Second Life.

'Sure it's just vibrations,' he told an audience at the 2006 Second Life Community Convention, 'but the vibrations plus the visuals plus the audio plus knowing that there's another person on the other end that you care about, or have talked to, or just met or clicked on their welcome area, you know they're there, you know it's real interaction versus just sitting there watching some porn.'

Hmm.

Where To Have Sex

A good place to get free casual poseball sex, if that's what you're into, is Nymphos Paradise. Here you will find sex of all kinds in all kinds of places. You can even have sex with a synthetic sheep; again, if that's what you're into. Nymphos Paradise is, apparently, 'a place for sexual and romantic fantasies to be lived out'. Owned and managed by sisters Lalinda Lovell and Lolita Lurra, Nymphos caters for just about every kind of fantasy or fetish you can imagine, including 'orgies, BDSM, ageplay, incest fantasy, rape fantasy, furry sex, bestiality fantasy, necro fantasy, forced feminization, adult babies, and medical/nurse fantasies'.

Unsurprisingly, if your avatar happens to be a woman, you'll find a lot more opportunities for sex with strangers. If being propositioned by one man after another is not what you're after, however, and you are a virtual woman, best steer clear of such places.

While we were here as a male avatar, we were propositioned by a member of Autumn Escorts. 'Looking for some fun?' we were asked. As it happens we were. Then, just as we were getting down to the tricky business of negotiation, our synthetic slattern was informed that there is no external escorting – or non-Nymphos whoring – allowed.

Thwarted. Thankfully, there are many other places where prostitution is rife. A quick search for the rather quaint term 'Escorts' will point you in the right direction.

Weapons

Second Life can be a violent place – as long as you stick to the designated areas. If you're keen to tool up or go postal, you'll soon learn that weapons work in much the same way as all accessories in Second Life. You acquire them, attach them to the relevant part of your body (generally hands), and start using them. Many weapons work using the mouselook command to allow accurate aiming and then a left mouse-click to fire.

The array of weapons available in-world is truly astonishing. From simple handguns and automatic weapons to elaborate missile launchers, tanks, and even nuclear weapons, all human death is there. Some weapons are designed just to maim (baseball bats, for example) or to knock your opponent a few metres across the sim – avatars do not bleed in Second Life (unless the victim has made their own cool animation) – while others are capable of inflicting a proper kill. Which in-world means you're teleported back to your home sim and have to teleport all the way back if you want to continue the fight.

There are also regular arms fairs where designers can show off their wares to eager shoppers. But if you want to slay on a shoestring, there are also plenty of free weapons caches lying around, although they're usually much weaker – and less fun to use – than their paid-for counterparts.

The ultimate Second Life weapon?

Although you could go giddy trying to get your head around the dazzling variety of weapons available to blow the hell out of your fellow Residents, there's one that we're particularly fond of. The nuclear bomb suitcase.

For a mere (and terrifying) L$500, you can own your very own piece of atomic luggage. Open the lid, set the timer (for anything up to two hours), leave the case lying around, and ... tick, tick, tick .... BOOM. Now just stand back and admire your mushroom.

Super.

A final warning

Although playing with weapons in Jessie and in the various weapons-permitted sandboxes is, of course, allowed, it's very, very important to remember to put your gun away before you fly or teleport back to the safe areas of the Grid. A couple of times we've found ourselves wandering around the Reuters building, or the petting zoo, completely forgetting that we're holding an Uzi. Easily done. But carrying a weapon in public is an excellent way to get yourself booted out of a sim, or even suspended from the entire Grid.

Gambling and Gaming

Unlike the games in the 'Sport, Leisure, and Games' chapter (p. 99), these in-world distractions come with the added fun of potentially taking all your Linden dollars. Or giving you loads more. New casinos are appearing – and old ones disappearing – all the time. To find the current crop of most popular ones, use the Second Life search panel, choose the 'places' tab and search for 'casino'. Alternatively, use the 'popular places' tab – there are always three or four casinos on the top-ten list that are worth visiting. A warning: many contain adult material.

Popular in-world casinos

Grande Sportsbook and Casino

Gambling, we can all agree, is a mug's game. Unless you win, in which case it's easy money. But if you're going to insist on frittering away your hard-earned Linden dollars on sports that you don't really understand the rules of, then there are few places better than the Grande Sportsbook and Casino. Offering betting on a variety of American sports, particularly NFL football, plus a casino with all the usual card games, you'll be losing your shirt faster than you can say, 'I'll see your L$100 and rez you two.'

Red Dragon Casino

If you like your casinos nice and seedy, the Red Dragon is the place for you. Escorts and all other kinds of loose avatar women vie for attention with blackjack, slots, and all that jazz. The music isn't half bad either. The only downside – or maybe it's an upside – is the persistent rumour that the entire joint is in cahoots with the Second Life Mafia, a rumour that the casino's recent torching to the ground did little to dispel.

Gold Rush Casino

Another popular Second Life gambling den, the Gold Rush boasts a huge variety of games in an environment designed, apparently, to mirror the red-carpeted windowless soul-vacuums of Las Vegas. A little less sleazy looking than the Red Dragon. But only a little.

A word on legality

Following a crackdown in the United States on online gambling sites, which has led to many closing and their owners being charged with criminal offences, there has been some debate about gambling areas in Second Life. The debate centres around the question of whether gambling with Linden dollars is the same as gambling with real dollars.

The position taken by Linden Lab is clear – the company does not provide gambling services or promote or support gambling in-world. It simply provides a platform for development that Residents are free to use in their own ways.

Therefore, for the purposes of the law, policing potential gambling in Linden dollars isn't its responsibility. However, it remains the case that there is a variety of ways to convert your Linden dollars back into real-world money, including the LindeX service provided by Linden Lab itself, which means gambling in Linden dollars can certainly boost – or deplete – your real-world bank account.

At the time of writing, there has been no test case or legislation to ascertain the legality of gambling in-world – but it's safe to say that while you're probably OK to have a flutter yourself, if you're thinking about setting up your own casino, you'll probably want to talk to a lawyer first.

Chapter Ten:
Useful Second Life Websites

As we've said before, with Second Life growing as fast as it is, any guidebook is doomed to be outdated the very second the final word is written. It's possible that by the time you read about them, some of the attractions mentioned in this book will have changed beyond all recognition or closed down entirely. And it's an absolute certainty that a whole load of new places will have appeared, many of which will be worthy of your attention.

But as luck would have it, the Internet is bursting at the seams with websites dedicated to Second Life and all its many subsets. In this section we provide a rundown of a few of the most popular. Bookmark these and you'll never be stuck for ideas on how to spend your in-world time.

http://secondlife.com

The obvious first click for budding Second Life Residents. Download the software, read the handy getting-started tutorials, find out what events are happening in-world, and discuss all things Second Life with other users. You'll be spending a lot of time here.

For Teen Second Life see **teen.secondlife.com**.

The Unofficial Tourists' Guide to Second Life Blog – http://www.unofficialsecondlife.com

The blog of this book. If you'll forgive its cheeky inclusion near the top of the list, we'll be keeping this blog up to date with any changes that we notice (or that you send in – **changes@unofficialsecondlife.com**) that affect the book. Here you'll also find a handy clickable list of all of the sims, places, and sites mentioned in the book. Just click and go.

Slurl.com – http://slurl.com

Short for Second Life URL, Slurl.com allows Second Life builders to provide direct hyperlinks to places within the Grid. Once you've entered your location into Slurl.com, the site will generate a direct teleport link that you can then post on the web or email to your friends to allow them to fly straight in and admire your handiwork.

Second Life Insider – http://www.secondlifeinsider.com

For a much more in-depth look beneath the surface of Second Life, you won't do much better than the Second Life Insider. With its close monitoring of new Second Life software features and interviews with notable Residents, it's a great way to go from noob to pro in a few weeks.

Second Life Herald – http://www.secondlifeherald.com

Second Life's favourite tabloid newspaper, the *Second Life*

Herald takes a chatty, sometimes snarky look at in-world life. Taking the format of a blog, the site is a great way to keep up to date with what's going on in Second Life, from a Resident's point of view.

New World Notes – http://nwn.blogs.com

The blog of Second Life expert Wagner James Au, *New World Notes* is a gateway to the coolest, most insider-y developments in-world. Features the great 'world from my window' feature where Residents share snapshots of the view from their in-world homes. (There is also a book of the same name already in production.)

Reuters in Second Life – http://secondlife.reuters.com

Reuters's in-world news centre is the online home of Adam Reuters, the world's first Real Life news agency-embedded Second Life journalist (see 'People', p. 57). Read Adam's reports and find out more about Reuters in Second Life here.

Second Life Total Arts and Entertainment – http://www.Slatenight.com

The Second Life Total Arts and Entertainment blog is the place to kick back, relax, and enjoy the more entertaining aspects of Second Life. From high-concept art to lowest-common-denominator music and clubbing, this is your link.

Second Seeker – http://secondseeker.com

'Tired of sex? Is clubbing boring? Let Second Seeker be your travel and cultural guide to the "no-sleaze" parts of Second Life.' So boasts the front page of **SecondSeeker.com**, the best guide to the prettier, cleaner parts in-world. Includes reviews covering architecture, health, museums, recreation and games, spiritual matters, and so much more.

SL Pics – http://www.sluniverse.com/pics
A nice feature of the Second Life software is the ability to record video or take snapshots in-world. It's a great way to record your most memorable SL experiences. SL Pics is a dedicated gallery to post and share your in-world photos with your fellow Residents.

Info Island – http://www.infoisland.org
The home of librarians on Second Life, Info Island provides virtual library services to Residents, helping to track down information of all sorts. A must for information junkies.

Eightbar – http://www.eightbar.co.uk
The home of Roo Reynolds, the man tasked by IBM to spend much of his first life in Second Life, exploring the possibilities of this brave new world and helping the company work out how to make the most of them. Roo's in-world involvements include the famed Second Life virtual Wimbledon tennis ground and tournament.

LindeX – http://secondlife.com/currency

The official Second Life currency exchange allows you to trade your Lindens for US dollars and vice versa.

SLBoutique – http://www.slboutique.com

Managed by the Electric Sheep Company (p. 120), SLBoutique is the web's biggest Second Life store, selling every single possible thing you could want for your avatar and your in-world home. From body parts and tattoos to soft furnishings, vehicles, and even pets, it's all here under one roof.

Linden Lifestyles – http://www.lindenlifestyles.com

The ultimate Second Life shopping blog, Linden Lifestyles is a fashion victim's dream. Updated daily with the latest in-world fashions – from clothing to jewellery.

The Electric Sheep Company – http://www.electricsheepcompany.com

One of the most influential Second Life developers, the Electric Sheep Company is responsible for many of the most ambitious Second Life builds, including the Nissan toast promotion, Democracy Island, and the Ben Folds Five in-world gig.

Aimee Weber – http://www.aimeeweber.com

Another Second Life developer icon, Aimee Weber is responsible for such in-world masterpieces as the Second Life Relay for Life, Midnight City, and the American Apparel Store.

Recommended Further Reading

This book is intended as a guidebook to the most interesting spots in Second Life and also as a primer to some of the skills and information you'll need to become a clued-up Resident. But it can't possibly offer everything you'll need to become an in-world expert. For that you'll need a much bigger book. A book like *Second Life: The Official Guide* by Michael Rymaszewski, Wagner James Au, Mark Wallace, and Catherine Winters.

Available from Amazon and all good bookshops.

Index of Topics